Essential
New
Zealand

by Allan Edie

PASSPORT BOOKS
NTC/Contemporary Publishing Company

Buskers in Cathedral Square, Christchurch

Page 1 *Shotover Jet, Queenstown*

Page 5a *rainforest fern*
5b: *New Zealand sheep*

Page15a: *surfers on Mount Maunganui beach*
15b: *Maori woodcarving, Rotorua*

Page 27a: *elaborate marae entrance*
27b: *Maori dancer*

Page 91a: *Maori warrior*
91b: *art deco architecture in Napier*

Page 117a: *flowers of the Pohutukawa tree*
117b: *Auckland pedicab*

Published by Passport Books, an imprint of NTC/
Contemporary Publishing Company, 4255 West
Touhy Avenue, Lincolnwood (Chicago), Illinois
60646–1975 U.S.A.

The contents of this publication are believed correct at
the time of printing. Nevertheless, the publishers cannot
accept responsibility for errors or omissions, nor for
changes in details given. We are always grateful to
readers who let us know of any errors or omissions
they come across, and future printings will be updated
accordingly.

Published by Passport Books in conjunction with
The Automobile Association of Great Britain.

Written by Allan Edie

Library of Congress Catalog Card Number: on file
ISBN 0–8442–0129–4

Color separation: BTB Digital Imaging, Whitchurch,
Hampshire

Printed and bound in Italy by Printer Trento srl

The weather chart on **page 118** of this book is
calibrated in °C. For conversion to °F simply use the
following formula:

$$°F = 1.8 \times °C + 32$$

Contents

About this Book

Essential *New Zealand* is divided into five sections to cover the most important aspects of your visit to New Zealand.

Viewing New Zealand pages 5–14
An introduction to New Zealand by the author.
> New Zealand's Features
> Essence of New Zealand
> The Shaping of New Zealand
> Peace and Quiet
> New Zealand's Famous

Top Ten pages 15–26
The author's choice of the Top Ten places in New Zealand, each with practical information.

What to See pages 27–90
The four main areas of New Zealand, each with its own brief introduction and an alphabetical listing of the main attractions.
> Practical information
> Snippets of 'Did You Know…' information
> 4 suggested walks
> 4 suggested tours
> 2 features

Where To… pages 91–116
Detailed listings of the best places to eat, stay, shop, take the children and be entertained.

Practical Matters pages 117–24
A highly visual section containing essential travel information.

Maps
All map references are to the individual maps found in the What to See section of this guide.
For example, Mount Cook National Park has the reference ✠ 62C2 – indicating the page on which the map is located and the grid square in which the National Park is to be found. A list of the maps that have been used in this travel guide can be found in the index.

Prices
Where appropriate, an indication of the cost of an establishment is given by £ signs:
£££ denotes higher prices, ££ denotes average prices, while £ denotes lower charges.

Star Ratings
Most of the places described in this book have been given a separate rating:
✪✪✪   Do not miss
✪✪   Highly recommended
✪   Worth seeing

Viewing
New
Zealand

Allan Edie's New Zealand

Early Travel
In the early 20th century, before the railway came through, the Wanganui River was promoted as 'New Zealand's Rhine'. Thus three days of river cruising, including a night spent on a houseboat miles from civilisation, became a fashionable way to travel.

Mitre Peak rises up dramatically from Milford Sound, Fiordland's best-known attraction

According to tradition, the early Polynesian Maori peoples were the first human beings to inhabit New Zealand, travelling to the islands in fleets of canoes during the 10th to 14th centuries. They were followed by European explorers and merchants, and later, in the 19th century, settlers and soldiers, gold-diggers and opportunists arrived. Today, tourists come from all over the world.

The New Zealand Tourism Board promotes the country as a 'real slice of Heaven', at 'the most beautiful end of the Earth'. To convince potential visitors that New Zealand is removed from the everyday hassles of the world; to explain that life here is how it used to be, and yet provide assurance that it is a thoroughly modern country with civilisation never far away; and to convince them that, despite occupying such a tiny area on a world map, it offers a tremendous variety of scenery and attractions, requires some degree of marketing skill.

To live in one of the world's most desirable holiday destinations is my good fortune for, with its easy-going lifestyle, clean, uncrowded environment, and spectacular landscapes ranging from volcanoes to glaciers, New Zealand surely is a favoured country.

New Zealand's Features

Petrified tree stumps litter the rock platform of Curio Bay in the Catlins region of the South Island

Time and Place
New Zealand lies in the temperate belt of the South Pacific Ocean; the 45th parallel (halfway between the Equator and the South Pole) passes through the South Island. In longitude it is almost exactly opposite the United Kingdom.

Standard time is 12 hours ahead of GMT; from mid-October until late March daylight-saving advances the time one hour.

Geography
The total area of New Zealand covers 270,000sq km, of which two major islands, the North and South Islands, just 25km apart, comprise 98 per cent. Although the South Island is a third larger than the North, the North claims three-quarters of the population – including the largest city, Auckland, with 1 million people, and the capital of Wellington. The South Island's leading city is Christchurch.

Stewart Island, 27km south of South Island, is the third largest land-mass, covering about 1,700sq km.

No part of New Zealand is further than 130km from the sea. The coastline, 5,650km long, includes many islands and estuaries.

The Climate
Summer lasts from December to February and fine autumn weather usually lasts through to May. During the winter months of June to August there is more rain in much of the country and snow falls occasionally in the high country of both the North and South Islands.

The People
The total population is 3.6 million, nearly 80 per cent of which is of European descent – mainly from Britain. The indigenous Polynesian people, known as Maori, comprise 12 per cent. Other South Pacific peoples and Asians make up most of the balance. Over 80 per cent of the population are urban dwellers.

Maori culture is evident throughout New Zealand: below, a carving from the Waitangi Meeting House, in Northland

7

Essence of New Zealand

The scenic beauty of New Zealand is well known. In many places the landscape is a dramatic mixture of mountains, glaciers, fiords and turbulent rivers, yet, in contrast, there are also gentle fields of grass, evergreen forests and quiet lakes. While for many visitors touring the countryside in a car or coach, or admiring the views through a window, glass in hand, is pleasure enough, over the last 20 years or so New Zealand has also become established as a centre for action, renowned for both 'soft' adventure and for more spectacular thrill experiences. Concern for the environment and a yearning for healthy pursuits has increased world-wide, making unspoilt New Zealand a popular destination for enjoying a host of outdoor activities.

White-water rafting at Rotorua, just one of the exciting sporting experiences New Zealand has to offer

THE **10** ESSENTIALS

If you only have a short time to visit New Zealand, or would like to get a really complete picture of the country, here are the essentials:

- **Visit a museum** – this is the number one tourist activity in New Zealand. Notable museums can be found in Auckland, Wellington, Christchurch and Dunedin, plus many other smaller towns.
- **Take a bush walk** – there are plenty of options ranging from 10-minute strolls to five-day treks. The temperate evergreen forest, never far away, is unique.
- **Stroll along a beach** – some are deserted, few are ever crowded.
- **Climb a mountain** – choose alpine ranges, bush-clad hills, active volcanoes or suburban viewpoints.
- **Inspect a thermal area** – marvel at bubbling mud and spouting geysers, or swim in hot water pools. There are thermal spas in many parts of the North Island and two in the South.
- **Watch a Maori concert** – be charmed by the dances and songs of the indigenous Maori people. And maybe follow it with a *hangi* (➤ 95).

- **Ride a jet-boat** – fast rides and fun rides on rivers and lakes are just one of the country's many 'thrill' experiences.
- **Watch a rugby match, or go horse-racing** – both exemplify the sporting passion of New Zealanders.
- **Drink the local wine or beer** – try a cool white wine, or an ice-cold beer: there are plenty of award winning labels to choose from, and plenty of places to try them!
- **Eat a New Zealand delicacy** – special delicacies to tempt your tastebuds include Bluff oysters or pavlova dessert.

Top: *the hot pools of the Waiotapu Thermal Reserve, near Rotorua*
Above: *Maori dancers putting on a show*

9

The Shaping of New Zealand

Tasman being attacked by native New Zealanders at Massacre Bay in 1642

AD 950
The legendary Polynesian explorer Kupe discovers New Zealand.

1150
Thought to be the approximate date for early Polynesian settlement.

1642
Dutchman Abel Tasman is the first European to discover New Zealand, but does not land.

1769
Famous English navigator Captain James Cook rediscovers New

Zealand. He later returns on two more voyages. After him came whalers, sealers and merchants, who exploited the country and its Maori inhabitants. The Bay of Islands becomes 'the hell-hole of the Pacific', with up to 40 sailing ships at a time stopping there.

1814
The first Christian missionary, Samuel Marsden, arrives. There are attempts to administer New Zealand from Australia.

1840
Captain Hobson, dispatched by the British government, arrives to initiate a treaty with the Maori and install British law. This Treaty of Waitangi still causes controversy today with its different English and Maori interpretations. Auckland was selected as the country's capital.

Recognition of British sovereignty: Maori chiefs sign the Treaty of Waitangi

1845
Battles occur in the Bay of Islands area between British troops and local Maori.

1848
Dunedin is settled under the auspices of the Free Church of Scotland.

1860s
The North Island land wars take place between British troops and Maori in the Waikato and Taranaki areas.

1861
Gold is discovered in Otago, inland from Dunedin. Further gold-rushes occur on the West Coast of the South Island and around the Thames-Coromandel area of the North Island.

1865
The capital is transferred from Auckland to Wellington, where it remains to this day.

1876
Having been temporarily established in 1867, Maori seats in Parliament were made permanent.

1882
First export of frozen meat to Britain. Supplying food to Britain becomes an important trade.

1886
Eruption of Mount Tarawera near Rotorua destroys three villages.

1887
The North Island volcanic peaks are given by local Maori to the New Zealand government; the area becomes the world's second national park.

1893
Women are permitted to vote in national elections.

1908
Auckland and Wellington are linked by rail across the North Island.

1919
Women are permitted to stand for Parliament.

'This way for gold': early prospectors flocked to the town of Ross at the turn of the century

1928
The first aeroplane flight between New Zealand and Australia takes place.

1931
The Hawke's Bay earthquake shatters the cities of Napier and Hastings, killing 256 people.

1935
An elected Labour government starts to introduce the Welfare State, with various social measures.

1953
The first tour of the country by a reigning monarch, Queen Elizabeth II, takes place.

1983
The signing of a Closer Economic Relations agreement with Australia.

1984
The Labour government commences the reforming and restructuring of the New Zealand economy.

1991
A Resource Management Act is passed, becoming the first environmental legislation of its kind in the world.

1996
The first national elections are held under a mixed member proportional system, resulting in a new-style coalition government.

Peace & Quiet

Noted British naturalist Dr David Bellamy has referred to New Zealand as 'Moa's Ark' – the moa (now extinct) being one of the country's indigenous flightless birds and ark being a reference to the country's split from the supposed Gondwana super-continent, including Australia and Antarctica, some 80 million years ago.

A Land Apart

For millions of years, until the arrival of man about 1,000 years ago, New Zealand was totally isolated from the rest of the world and a unique collection of plants and animals flourished undisturbed. Among these are the flightless birds which evolved because ground-dwelling mammals (their predators) had not reached New Zealand at the time of the split.

Guided walks can be taken on the spectacular Fox (below) and Franz Josef glaciers

Man's presence, with consequent agriculture and defor- estation, has undoubtedly had a great impact on the country's wildlife over the last few hundred years, but despite this a vast number of fascinating species has survived.

A Protected Landscape

These days the natural landscape and its flora and fauna are well protected and New Zealand has 13 national parks, comprising 3 million hectares – 11 per cent of its land area. In addition there are three maritime parks, 20 forest parks and nearly 4,000 other nature and scenic reserves.

Mountains rise to 3,754m. Indeed, three-quarters of the land area is above 200m in altitude. Glaciers, fiords, lakes and rivers decorate the interior. The rich native evergreen forest provides splendid cover and the native birdlife population remains large, albeit reduced from yesteryear.

Some Specialities

The kiwi is probably the most well-known bird because it is both a symbol of New Zealand and the name often applied to the country's human residents. Unfortunately its nocturnal nature, along with reduced numbers, means that visitors rarely see it in its natural surroundings, although birds are on display at several zoos and aviaries.

The beautiful white herons return to their sole breeding colony – the trees of south Westland – each summer, and a special hide allows visitors to observe and photograph them. Penguins waddle ashore at several South Island sites under the watchful gaze of a grandstand of tourists.

The tuatara is a rare lizard-like animal related to the dinosaur, but there are a few places where they can be observed. More accessible is the sea-life: go whale watching, or swim with dolphins.

New Zealand's most famous flightless bird, the kiwi, although it is rarely seen in the wild

Enjoying and Conserving

Peace and quiet abounds in the New Zealand countryside. There are plenty of picnic sites away from the crowds and plenty of bush walks to either amble around in solitude or undertake with friends; there are rivers to fish and mountains to climb. Within an hour or so of wherever you are, there will be a choice of places to get away from it all.

An important facet of New Zealand tourism is its commitment to looking after the interests of both visitors and the environment and the conservation authorities perform a credible task at managing this fickle relationship; so, while visitors are invited to enjoy the countryside, they are also asked not to exploit or destroy it.

New Zealand's Famous

*National heroine
Jean Batten,
commemorated on a
cigarette card*

Jean Batten (1909–82)

A world famous aviatrix, Batten became the first woman to fly solo from England to Australia, in 1934. In 1936 she was the first person to fly solo from England to New Zealand, taking 11 days.

Sir Peter Blake (1949–)

Born in Auckland, Sir Peter became a renowned international yachtsman following his victory in the Whitbread round-world race, his record-breaking trip around the world in a catamaran, and his victory of the America's Cup for New Zealand in 1995.

Father of Nuclear Physics
Scientist Ernest Rutherford, born near Nelson, went to Cambridge in England after studying at Christchurch University. The most famous achievement in his long and distinguished career was discovering how to split the atom. On his death in 1937 Rutherford was buried in Westminster Abbey, in London, having been knighted and made a peer.

Sir Edmund Hillary (1919–)

Hillary is recognised as perhaps the country's most respected hero. He was the first man to conquer Mount Everest – in 1953 – and has been involved with other Himalayan and Antarctic expeditions.

Katherine Mansfield (1888–1923)

Internationally known short-story writer Katherine Mansfield chose Wellington, where she was born, as the location for many of her stories.

Dame Ngaio Marsh (1899–1982)

Famous as a detective-story writer, Dame Ngaio was born in Christchurch. In addition to her writing, she was involved with Shakespearean productions in both the United Kingdom and New Zealand.

Dame Kiri Te Kanawa (1944–)

Dame Kiri, New Zealand's most famous opera soprano, born in Gisborne, is now mainly resident in London. Although renowned as a leading opera singer, she has also produced several albums of lighter music.

Top Ten

1
Abel Tasman National Park

🞤 63E5

✉ Northwest of Nelson, via SH60

☎ 03 528 6543 (Motueka visitor information)

🕐 Year round

🍴 Awaroa Lodge (££); no road access

🚌 Daily tour bus from Nelson

🛳 Ferries from Kaiteriteri & Nelson

♿ Few; not suitable

✋ Free access

❓ Reduced transport facilities in winter

Easy, level walking and lovely coastal scenery makes Abel Tasman a firm favourite with hikers

Near the top of the South Island, this is neither New Zealand's largest nor grandest national park, but remains one of the most popular.

The park, named after the first European discoverer of New Zealand, Abel Tasman, lies close to Motueka, west of the city of Nelson. Its coastal location offers a great combination of bush and deserted beach but it really needs to be explored on foot as road access is limited. The gentle and very popular coastal track, one of the easiest and most beautiful in the country, takes about four days to complete; plan and watch out for tides if cutting cross the sands. There are national park huts available for accommodation along the way and tickets for these should be purchased before setting out. Launch services also serve the coastal bays so walkers can tackle short sections at a time if they wish.

Inland, the higher areas of the park are more rugged, the landscape a mixture of limestone and marble contours. Canaan and Harwoods Hole in particular contrast with the bush and beach at sea level.

There are two other national parks in this area. The Kahurangi Park (▶ 72) in the northwest of the Nelson region features the well-known Heaphy Track, which takes four to five days to complete, while the Nelson Lakes National Park (▶ 74) in the south of the region is known for the twin lakes of Rotoiti (where there is a visitor centre) and Rotoroa. Surrounded by mountains and forests, the lakes offer boating, fishing, picnic sites and gentle strolls. For the more energetic and experienced, there are spectacular high-country tracks.

2
Cape Reinga

A lighthouse at Cape Reinga, New Zealand's northernmost point, guards the rippling waters of the Tasman Sea and the Pacific Ocean.

From the promontory there are spectacular views to the left and right as the coast sweeps away in a combination of cliffs and sand-dunes. This is the legendary departure point for the spirits of the dead Maori people returning to their heavenly homeland of 'Hawaiki'.

Part of the thrill of a visit to Cape Reinga is the journey there. It is situated 116km north of Kaitaia and 220km north of Paihia – the two most popular stepping-off points. The journey there and back can easily be driven, but coach tours (taking a day) are very popular because they include a 60km-stretch along Ninety Mile Beach, the sands that run down the west side of the peninsula. Although motorists

✚	32A5
✉	Northern tip of the North Island, via SH1
☎	09 408 0879 (Kaitaia visitor information)
🕐	Year round
🍴	Waitiki Landing (££); 18km from Cape
🚌	Daily tours from Kaitaia & Paihia
♿	Good to viewpoint
✋	Free access

in private cars are permitted to drive along this beach (actually 90km long, not 90 miles), it is forbidden to do so in rental vehicles. Access at the northern end, connecting the beach and the road near the Cape, is via a stream-bed with quicksand and coaches are the only vehicles permitted to traverse it.

Coach tours also stop at the Wagener Museum at Houhora. Here there is a large collection of Victorian bric-à-brac plus several Maori exhibits. Next door is the Subritzky Homestead, an early pioneer house.

Commercial facilities on Cape Reinga are extremely limited, although it is possible to post a letter there. More amenities are located 18km away at Waitiki Landing.

Ninety Mile Beach (actually 56 miles) runs down the west side of the Northland peninsula

3
Fiordland National Park

82B3

At the end of SH94, north of Te Anau

03 249 8900 (Te Anau visitor information)

Tour coach to Milford Sound departs Te Anau 10AM; also 8AM in summer. Access & options reduced in winter

Hotel dining room & bistro at Milford (££)

Day tours from Te Anau & Queenstown

Milford Sound: several launches daily (with meals on board)

Scheduled & scenic flights from Queenstown to Milford Sound with Mount Cook Airlines (03 442 2670)

Good boardwalk at Milford Sound

Free access

Day tour from Queenstown (► 79)

Below: *the aptly named Mirror Lakes*

The Fiordland National Park is not only the largest national park in New Zealand, but one of the largest in the world.

In contrast to the coastline at the north of the South Island, where the Marlborough Sounds offer a gentle landscape of bush-clad hills and meandering sea passages, the sounds of the Fiordland National Park in the south are rugged, glacier-carved fiords with deep waters and precipitous sides. Inland, behind the jagged coastline, is an impenetrable region of bush-clad hills, deep lakes and high mountains covering some 12,000sq km, where rare species of wildlife have managed to survive undisturbed. In addition, the high annual rainfall results in dozens of dramatic waterfalls.

The most northerly of the fiords is Milford Sound, and the road leading to it is one of the highlights of the park. It is also possible to fly to the sound, or walk to it along the Milford Track (► 89) over a period of four days. Most of the other fiords are inaccessible other than by sea.

A launch trip on the sound is highly recommended and, regardless of the weather, the spectacle of the sheer cliffs dropping down 1,200m to the water provide dramatic scenery of the grandest order.

The trip through to Doubtful Sound via Lake Manapouri (▶ 88) and the Wilmot Pass must rate a close second. Winter cruises lasting four to five days can be taken to some of the other sounds.

Right beside Lake Te Anau, the South Island's largest lake, is the township of the same name; it is commonly known as the 'gateway' to the national park (▶ 90).

Above: *a well-known walking track follows the Hollyford Valley, the longest in Fiordland, to the coast at Martins Bay*

Left: *sheer rock rises up on either side of the Cleddau Valley*

19

4
Harrah's Auckland Sky Tower

The view over the city and harbour from this tall observation tower is immense. Conversely, the tower is visible from anywhere in Auckland.

✚ 36B2

✉ Corner of Victoria & Federal streets

☎ 09 912 6000

🕐 Year round

🍴 Bar & bistro (££) at 220m level

♿ Good

✋ Moderate

❓ Walking tour of central Auckland (➤ 37)

Crowned by its needle-like mast, the Sky Tower soars above the rest of Auckland's buildings

Outstripping Sydney's AMP Tower (304m) or the Paris Eiffel Tower (320m), at 328m the Sky Tower is the tallest structure in the southern hemisphere and ranks seventh in the world. Set on a rise above the central business district, it dominates the Auckland skyline.

The tower has two enclosed circular observation decks and an open deck 220m up, plus a revolving bar and a bistro-style restaurant providing a full 360-degree view of Auckland every 60 minutes. One of the observation decks is available for private functions. Fast lifts, three of them glass-fronted, make access to the tower possible. Up to 850 people can be accommodated in the tower at any one time.

The top six floors house communication facilities and a mast handles VHF, UHF, AM and FM broadcasting and telecommunications transmissions.

The Casino at the base of the tower is the largest in New Zealand (there is only one other), with 1,050 gaming machines and 100 gaming tables. The complex also includes a 344-room hotel, four restaurants, a theatre and a convention centre.

5
Mount Cook National Park

New Zealand's highest peak, Mount Cook, forms the centrepiece of this beautiful alpine area in the heart of the South Island.

Much of the South Island is mountainous and the Southern Alps mountain range forms a backbone for most of the island's length. Of some 220 named peaks over 2,300m in New Zealand, the highest, at 3,754m, commemorates the famous English navigator who first landed in New Zealand in 1769. It was known to the Maoris as Aoraki, after a mythical god. Near by, Mount Tasman, in second place, rises to 3,498m.

Mount Cook lies in the 70,000-hectare Mount Cook National Park, adjacent to the Westland National Park on the western side of the Alps. These two parks, together with Mount Aspiring (➤ 90) and Fiordland (➤ 18) national parks, have been incorporated into a World Heritage area.

Most of the Mount Cook National Park is alpine terrain favoured by trekkers and climbers and the mountains offer a spectacular panorama of peaks, glaciers and rivers from a number of marked tracks of varying difficulty. Full information is available from the park's visitor centre. Flights in ski-equipped light aircraft are a popular option, taking in views of Mount Cook and the Alps, and including a landing on the snowfield of the Tasman Glacier. At 28km long, it is the longest of any glacier in the world's temperate zones.

The majority of South Island coach tours visiting the park include Mount Cook village (also known as The Hermitage, after the well-known hotel there) on the itinerary, either looping in as a day trip, or spending a night or two there.

62C2

At the end of SH80, 333km west of Christchurch

03 435 1818

Daily 8–5 (Mount Cook visitor information)

Dining facilities at Mount Cook hotels (££)

Buses from Christchurch & Queenstown

Flights from Christchurch & Queenstown

Few paths suitable

Free access

Mount Cook rising up beyond Lake Pukaki, which is fed by the Tasman Glacier and the Tasman River

6
Queenstown's Skyline Gondola

One of the highlights of the South Island's premier tourist centre is a ride high above the town on the Skyline Gondola.

✚ 82C4

✉ Brecon Street, Queenstown

☎ 03 442 7860

🕓 9AM–10PM

🍴 Café & restaurant morning to evening

♿ Few; check

✋ Moderate

❓ Queenstown (➤ 79)

The many attractions of Queenstown and its surrounding area are featured later in the book (➤ 79), but one of the most enjoyable things to do, and a good way to get your bearings, is to take a ride on the Skyline Gondola cableway, which opened in 1967. The base terminal is a 15-minute walk from Queenstown's shops.

The ride itself, lasting just four minutes, takes visitors 450m up a steep hillside in small cabins suspended from overhead cables. From the viewing platform at the top of the hill the splendid views not only encompass the town below, but stretch out across glittering Lake Wakatipu to the surrounding snow-capped mountains of the Remarkables range.

The complex at the upper terminal includes a restaurant and a wide-screen cinema where an entertaining short film, *Kiwi Magic*, is shown at regular intervals throughout the day. The film takes viewers on a tour of New Zealand's finest scenery by various means of transport, including biplane and jet-boat.

View of the upper terminal, the town and Lake Wakatipu from one of the Skyline's cable cars

7
Tongariro National Park

This sacred 'land of fire', given by the Maori to the New Zealand government over 100 years ago, is now a Unesco recognised World Heritage reserve.

Lake Rotoaura, at the northern end of the park

Lying at the centre of the North Island's volcanic plateau is the island's highest mountain – the active volcanic peak of Mount Ruapehu (2,797m). Adjacent to it are Mount Ngauruhoe (2,291m) and Mount Tongariro (1,968m) and together the trio form the heart of a high and sometimes bleak area known as the Tongariro National Park. The land was given to the government by the Maori tribal owners in 1887, and it became New Zealand's first – and the world's second – national park.

Tongariro is now New Zealand's most popular national park, mainly because of its excellent ski areas, namely the Whakapapa ski field which lies on the northern slopes of Mount Ruapehu (25km from a small community called National Park), and the Turoa field on the southwestern slopes (served by the town of Ohakune). The ski season generally runs from about late June to September – sometimes longer.

Ruapehu is an active volcano with a warm crater lake and although normally placid, there were eruptions in 1995 and 1996. Cone-shaped Ngauruhoe periodically emits a cloud of steam, but rarely erupts. Tongariro is dormant, but has a hot spring on its slopes.

There are many walking tracks through the park, including the Tongariro Crossing, a popular full-day trek across the shoulders of Mount Tongariro. For those fit enough, it is possible to make a side trip to the top of Tongariro, or even to Ngauruhoe.

✚ 50B3

✉ At the end of SH48, off SH47 between SH1 and SH4

☎ 07 892 3729 (Whakapapa visitor information)

🕐 Year round (subject to winter snow)

🍴 Grand Chateau (££) is the main hotel

🚌 Through National Park & Ohakune

🚉 National Park & Ohakune rail stations

♿ Few paths; accessible if accompanied

✋ Free access

↔ Taupo (➤ 45)

❓ Ski tours in winter from Auckland

8
TranzAlpine Express

🕂 63D2

✉ Christchurch Station, Addington

☎ 0800 802802 (freephone)

🕐 Depart 9AM, return arrival 6:35PM

🍴 Refreshments available on train (£)

🚂 Christchurch station; also Greymouth railway station

♿ Few; assistance required

✋ Expensive

↔ Christchurch (➤ 64)

Approaching Arthur's Pass, the highpoint of the train journey through the Southern Alps

Crossing the Southern Alps via mountain passes, tunnels and viaducts, this single-track line links the east and west coasts of the South Island.

One of the success stories of the privately owned railway system in New Zealand has been the promotion of the train from Christchurch, through the Southern Alps mountains, to the west coast town of Greymouth. Marketed as the TranzAlpine, it has become a very popular tourist service, either as a one-way link between the coasts, or as a round-trip excursion from Christchurch. The narrow-gauge train is diesel-hauled and the carriages have large picture windows; there is also a special carriage with open sides for viewing.

Departing daily from Christchurch in the morning, the train first crosses the neat and tidy farmlands of the Canterbury Plains, passing through a number of small towns before stopping at Springfield. From here the journey is particularly spectacular as the train continues across viaducts and through tunnels across the Canterbury foothills up to Arthur's Pass. At 737m, this is the highest railway station in the South Island and sees the arrival of many hikers bound for Arthur's Pass National Park.

Shortly after halting here the train enters the 8-km Otira Tunnel for the descent of 259m to Otira. Now on the other side of the Alps, the rainforests and scrubby landscapes of Westland offer a contrast in scenery to the eastern side. The line continues past mountains and along river valleys before running alongside the Grey River into Greymouth. The train returns to Christchurch in the afternoon.

9

Waitomo Caves

These are one of New Zealand's greatest natural wonders, where glow-worms twinkle like stars on the roof of a cave above an underground river.

The caves are situated some 200km south of Auckland and can be found along a side road between the towns of Otorohanga and Te Kuiti. There are a number of rocky outcrops, with a labyrinth of caves and channels beneath, in the area.

The two main caves open to the public here are the Waitomo Caves and the Aranui Cave – though the former, which have given their name to the area, are the more popular. Visitors in guided parties are led through subterranean chambers of varying sizes containing delicate limestone stalactite and stalagmite formations highlighted by special lighting effects.

The main feature of the Waitomo Caves, however, is the dinghy ride along an underground stream into a cave where, in the darkness, one can gaze up at thousands of glow-worms lighting up the roof like stars in the sky. The effect is created by the 'lights' that these tiny insects have to lure prey into their mesh of sticky mucus threads.

The Aranui Cave is worth visiting for its beautiful limestone formations, although it does not have the attraction of a glow-worm grotto. Both caves are usually very busy with coach tour groups in the middle of the day so avoid this time if at all possible.

Near the Waitomo Caves, the Museum of Caves provides good audio-visual displays and shows about the glow-worms, while on the road leading out to Waitomo the Ohaki Maori Village gives an interesting insight into the Maori culture and way of life. With the exception of a hotel, facilities near the caves are limited.

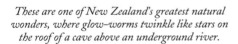

🚩 32C1

✉ 8km off SH3, south of Otorohanga

☎ 07 878 7640 (Waitomo visitor information)

🕐 Daily, half-hourly, 9AM–4:30PM

🍴 Waitomo Hotel (££)

🚌 Minibus transfers from intercity buses

🚉 Transfers from Otorohanga station

♿ None

✋ Moderate

❓ Included in most North Island coach tours

Lighting brings the limestone formations of the Waitomo Caves to life

10
Whakarewarewa Thermal Reserve

If you can only get to see one attraction in the Rotorua region, then 'Whaka' (as the reserve is commonly known) should be it.

✚ 33D1

✉ Tryon Street or Hemo Road

☎ 07 348 9047

🕐 Daily 8–5

🍴 No dining in grounds

🚌 Minibus transfers from Rotorua visitor centre

🅿 Rotorua

♿ Few; assistance required

✋ Moderate

↔ Rotorua (➤ 42)

❓ Guides available

The city of Rotorua (➤ 42), near the centre of the North Island, is renowned for its volcanic activity evidenced by spouting geysers, bubbling mud and a pervasive smell of hydrogen sulphide. The area is surrounded by forest, has a dormant volcano and over a dozen lakes, plus many other attractions. It is also a centre for a display of Maori culture.

About 3km from the city centre, Whakarewarewa is Rotorua's most famous thermal area, of which there are a total of five in the region. It features the Pohutu (Maori for 'splashing') geyser which spouts up 30m high at regular intervals and the smaller Prince of Wales Feathers geyser (reaching 12m), which always erupts first. Near by are steaming cauldrons of bubbling mud and strange, moonscape-like silica formations.

Overlooking the thermal area of Whaka is a re-creation of a palisaded *pa*, or fortress, such as that used by Maori warriors in earlier days. Also close by is the Maori Arts and Crafts Institute, established in the 1960s, where the cultural skills of the Maori people are demonstrated and their work displayed. There is a souvenir shop and a concert of Maori action songs is presented daily at 12:15PM inside the Te Aronui a Rua Meeting House.

Quite close to the Whakarewarewa reserve is a grove of Redwood trees which offers a shady walk and provides a contrast to the many thousands of acres of pine trees which cover the 'volcanic plateau' around Rotorua.

The Prince of Wales Feathers geyser

What To See

NEW ZEALAND

4 — Cape Reinga
Kaitaia
Kaikohe
Whangarei
Dargaville
Great Barrier I
Coromandel Peninsula
Coromandel
AUCKLAND
Manukau
East Cape

North Island

Hamilton
Te Kuiti
Bay of Plenty
Tauranga
Whakatane
Rotorua
Gisborne

3 — **New Plymouth**
Cape Egmont
Lake Taupo
Taupo
2797m
Mt Ruapehu
Wairoa
Napier
Hawke Bay
2518m
Mt Egmont
Wanganui
Hastings
Palmerston North
Levin
Masterton

Cape Farewell
Motueka
Tasman Bay
Nelson
Picton
Cook Strait
Lower Hutt
WELLINGTON

South Island
Westport
Blenheim
Reefton
2338m
Greymouth
Kaikoura

2 — Hokitika
Southern Alps
Pegasus Bay
3754m
Mt Cook
Christchurch
Banks Peninsula
Ashburton
Canterbury Bight
3027m
Waitaki
Timaru
Milford Sound
Queenstown
Oamaru
Lake Te Anau
L. Wakatipu
Te Anau
Clutha

1 — **Dunedin**
Balclutha
Invercargill
Foveaux Strait
Stewart Island

0   200   400 km

A   B   C

The terraced slopes of once-fortified Mount Eden, Auckland's highest volcanic peak, are still clearly visible

Upper North Island

This quarter of New Zealand, which includes its largest city, Auckland, is home to over half the country's population. It is also the main gateway to the rest of the country.

Stretching to the north of Auckland is the narrow peninsula known as Northland, the birthplace of European settlement. Lonely Cape Reinga, at the far northern tip, is where the ancient Maori spirits of the dead are supposed to have left to return to their Polynesian home. In contrast is the busy resort area of the Bay of Islands on the east coast.

About three hours' drive to the southeast of Auckland is the famous tourist city of Rotorua, with its geothermal attractions and displays of Maori culture set amid forest and lakes. Still further south, in the North Island's centre, is the resort township of Taupo, nestled on the shore of the country's largest lake and with a distant view of the brooding volcanoes of Tongariro National Park.

' Auckland – Last, loneliest, loveliest, exquisite, apart. '

RUDYARD KIPLING
The Song of the Cities
(1893)

Auckland

The city, built over the dormant remnants of some 50 volcanoes, sprawls across a narrow isthmus between the Pacific Ocean and the Tasman Sea, beach and bush both readily at hand. With a population of 1 million, it is New Zealand's largest and most cosmopolitan city as well as being the main commercial and industrial centre. In addition, Auckland offers an array of cultural activities.

Auckland is the major New Zealand gateway for both air and sea passengers and there are road, rail and coach services to most parts of the North Island.

European settlement began here in 1840 and it was New Zealand's capital until 1865. The compact downtown area is still its hub, but there are major shopping and entertainment areas beyond the central streets, and the attractions for tourists spread into the suburbs.

Auckland Bridge spanning the harbour with Stanley Bay in the distance

For those wanting to get away from the hustle and bustle of the city, in addition to its two harbours and gulf islands – the multitude of yachts always bobbing about in the Hauraki Gulf has given the city its nickname 'City of Sails' – Auckland offers extensive regional reserves, a 'new' volcanic island, a gannet colony, both white and black sand beaches and a forest backdrop.

What to See in Auckland

ALBERT PARK ⭐
Conveniently located close to the central district's main street, this formal garden features a Victorian pavilion and statuary among its flowerbeds and trees. It is well used as a shady retreat by both office workers and students from the adjacent university campus.

- 36B2
- Princes Street
- 09 373 4455
- Unrestricted
- Few
- Free access

AOTEA CENTRE ⭐
Situated on central Aotea Square, the building houses a visitor information bureau, a concert hall and a conference centre, exhibition areas, restaurants and bars. There is also a booking office for most Auckland events: check what's on during your stay.

The Auckland Town Hall, the city's original town hall, built in 1911, has been restored and now serves as another concert venue. Its attractive clock tower makes a distinctive landmark.

- 36B2
- Aotea Square, Queen Street
- 09 309 2678
- Daily 8:30–5:30. Closed Sun
- Alberts Restaurant (££)
- Good

AUCKLAND HARBOUR BRIDGE ⭐
Arching across Waitemata Harbour (➤ 38) to the North Shore suburbs, the bridge is over 1km long and, at a height of 43m, allows shipping to pass beneath it. It was opened in 1959 with four lanes and later widened to eight. Harbour cruises go under it and sightseeing coaches go over it, but there is no pedestrian access.

- 36B3
- Views from Shelly Beach Road & Westhaven Drive; beware of one-way streets

AUCKLAND ZOO ⭐
Situated near the Museum of Transport, Technology and Social History (➤ 35), and connected to it by vintage tram, Auckland's zoo houses a selection of the usual overseas creatures plus native species such as the kiwi in a nocturnal house and indigenous birds in a forest aviary. There is a farm animal section for children and the whole complex features pleasant naturalistic compounds. At certain times the keepers give talks at various enclosures. It is New Zealand's largest and most extensive zoo.

- 36A2
- Motions Road, Western Springs
- 09 360 3819
- Daily 9:30–5:30; last admission 4:15
- Café (£)
- 045
- Good
- Cheap

31

UPPER NORTH ISLAND

0   2   4   6   8   100 km

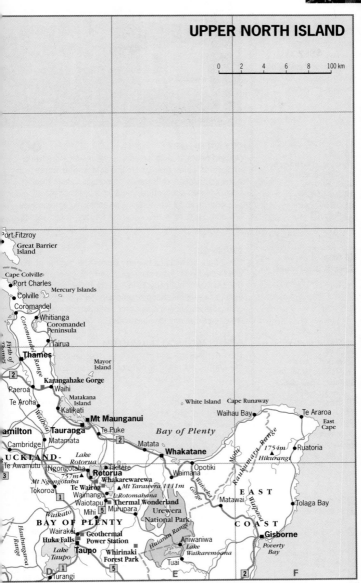

Port Fitzroy

Great Barrier Island

Cape Colville
Port Charles
Colville   Mercury Islands
Coromandel
Whitianga
Coromandel Peninsula
Tairua

Firth of Thames
Thames
Coromandel Range

2
Paeroa   Waihi
Te Aroha   Karangahake Gorge
Matakana Island
Katikati

Mayor Island

Mt Maunganui

amilton   **Tauranga**   Te Puke
Cambridge   Matamata   2   Matata   **Whakatane**
Waikato
UCKLAND-
Te Awamutu
Lake Rotorua
Ngongotaha   Tikitere
3
Mt Ngongotaha 757m   **Rotorua**
Tokoroa   Te Wairoa   Whakarewarewa
1   Waimangu   L.Rotomahana
Waiotapu   ▲ Mt Tarawera 1111m
Mihi   5   **Thermal Wonderland**
Murupara
BAY OF PLENTY
Wairakei
Huka Falls   Geothermal Power Station
Waikato
Haurungaroa Range
Lake Taupo
Taupo   Whirinaki Forest Park

White Island   Cape Runaway
Waihau Bay   Te Araroa
East Cape

Bay of Plenty

Opotiki
Waimana
Waioeka Gorge
EAST
Matawai
Tolaga Bay

Urewera National Park

Kaukumara Range

▲1754m
Hikurangi   Ruatoria

Huiarau Range
Aniwaniwa
Lake Waikaremoana
Tuai

C O A S T
Gisborne
Poverty Bay

1   5   D.   Turangi   E   2   F

Once threatened with demolition, this handsome building standing on the edge of Albert Park now houses the City Art Gallery

---

CITY ART GALLERY

Housed behind a Victorian edifice, the main gallery has an important collection of New Zealand and imported paintings, prints and drawings. Important touring displays from overseas also feature here (admission charge).

Opposite is the New Gallery, an annex of contemporary art, and close by is the Auckland Central Public Library which houses a collection of historic and rare books.

DEVONPORT ⭐⭐

Devonport, 10 minutes by ferry across the harbour at the end of the North Shore peninsula, is an attractive suburb of the city. With its many 19th-century buildings, it offers visitors a delightful shopping area consisting of bookshops, craft galleries, antique shops and cafés. Alternatively, there are three museums to choose from.

DOMAIN AND AUCKLAND MUSEUM ⭐⭐⭐

The extensive parkland of the Domain lies on the fringes of the central district. The Winter Gardens display exotic plants in a hot-house and there is also a dell of New Zealand ferns.

Foremost, however, is the impressive **Auckland Museum** housing extensive displays on the Maori and Polynesian cultures, the flora and fauna of New Zealand, arts and crafts from other countries, and a war memorial display. Special exhibitions are also frequently mounted.

HARRAH'S AUCKLAND SKY TOWER (▶ 20, TOP TEN)

HOBSON WHARF NATIONAL ⭐⭐
MARITIME MUSEUM

As an island nation, New Zealand has a considerable maritime heritage and this is innovatively displayed inside old warehouses next to the quayside near the foot of Queen Street. As well as traditional displays with exhibits ranging from Polynesian canoes to America's Cup yachts, there are a number of workshops where crafts such as

---

City Art Gallery
- 🕂 36B2
- ✉ Corner of Wellesley & Kitchener streets
- ☎ 09 307 7700
- 🕐 Daily 10–5
- 🍽 Gallery café (££)
- ♿ Good ◾ Free
- ❓ Free guided tour 2PM

Devonport
- 🕂 36C3
- ✉ North Shore Peninsula

Domain and Auckland Museum
- 🕂 36B2
- ✉ Auckland Domain
- ☎ Museum: 09 306 7067
- 🕐 Daily 10–5. Closed 25 Dec & Good Fri
- 🍽 Coffee shop (£)
- ♿ Few
- ◾ Free (charge for special exhibitions)
- ❓ Maori concerts 11AM & 1:30PM daily

Hobson Wharf National Maritime Museum
- 🕂 36B3
- ✉ Hobson Wharf, Quay Street
- ☎ 09 373 0800
- 🕐 Daily 9–6; 5 in winter
- 🍽 Light refreshments (£)
- ♿ Few ◾ Cheap
- ❓ Harbour cruises

Richard Pearce's first plane on show at MOTAT

sail-making and wood-carving are demonstrated, trips on an old steam launch, plus the marina at the centre of the complex where various craft are moored. Also shown is the importance of sea trade to the history and commerce of New Zealand.

KELLY TARLTON'S ANTARCTIC ENCOUNTER ✪✪✪
AND UNDERWATER WORLD

This popular 'walk-in' aquarium, named after a famous underwater diver, offers glass tunnels surrounded by fish and other marine animals, including sharks, from New Zealand waters.

A recent addition is a ride through a re-creation of an Antarctic landscape, with a replica of explorer Sir Robert Scott's hut, a colony of live penguins and an aquarium of life that exists below the Antarctic ice cap.

- 🕀 36C2
- ✉ Tamaki Drive, Okahu Bay
- ☎ 09 528 1994
- 🕐 Winter 9–6; summer 9–9
- 🍴 Kelly's café opposite (££)
- 🚌 Nos 72X to 76X
- ♿ Few; should be accompanied
- 💷 Moderate

MOUNT EDEN AND ONE TREE HILL ✪✪

Respectively the highest (196m) and second highest (183m) of Auckland's mainland volcanic peaks, both provide panoramic views although Mount Eden gives the closer view of Auckland's downtown and harbour areas. Roads go to the top of both, but most sightseeing coaches opt for Mount Eden.

Both were former Maori *pas* (fortresses) and terracing and storage pits are still visible.

- 🕀 36B2/C1
- ✉ Access off Hillside Crescent, Mount Eden Road; 4km from downtown
- 🕐 Unrestricted access
- 🍴 Langton's (££), on slopes
- ♿ Road to top
- 💷 Free access
- ❓ Road is partly one-way

MUSEUM OF TRANSPORT, TECHNOLOGY AND ✪
SOCIAL HISTORY

Often known by its acronym of 'MOTAT', this suburban museum, spread over two sites 1km apart, displays vintage cars, aircraft, trams, colonial buildings and other technological specimens from yesteryear, largely maintained by volunteer groups. Exhibits of interest include a replica of the Pearce aircraft which reputedly flew over the South Island at about the time (possibly even earlier) that the Wright brothers made their more famous first flight, and the only Solent Mark IV flying boat left in the world.

- 🕀 36A2
- ✉ Great North Road, Western Springs
- ☎ 09 846 7020
- 🕐 Daily 10–5. Closed 25 Dec
- 🍴 Refreshments & restaurant (££)
- 🚌 045
- ♿ Good 💷 Cheap
- ❓ Working weekends advertised occasionally

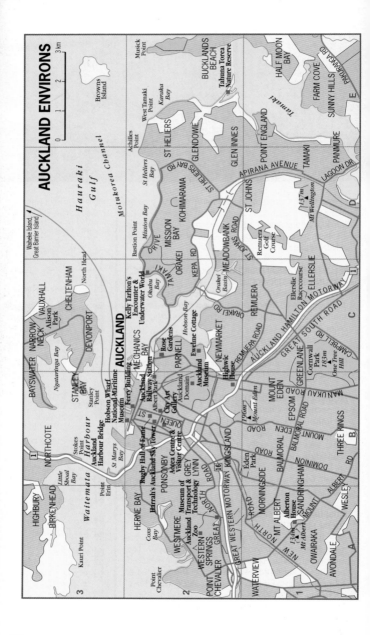

AUCKLAND ENVIRONS

A Walk Around Downtown Auckland

Attractions ranging from the Aotea Centre to a ride up the Sky Tower feature on this culturally interesting walk.

From Queen Elizabeth II Square walk eastwards along Quay Street. Turn into Britomart Place, past the bus terminal, then cross Customs Street and proceed to Emily Place. Take the steps in the reserve to Princes Street, passing the Hyatt Regency Hotel.

Albert Park, a popular lunchtime retreat in the heart of the city

The Governor-General's former residence, the Maclaurin Chapel and the Maidment Arts Theatre all form part of the extensive Auckland University.

Stroll through Albert Park (➤ 31) to the City Art Gallery (➤ 34).

A short block downhill is Queen Street. Note the Civic Theatre. Built in 1929, the Arabian designs inside are still eye-catching.

One block up Queen Street is Aotea Square. Cross the square to the Aotea Centre (➤ 31) and look within its atrium.

From the Aotea Centre, walk behind the Civic Theatre, along brick-surfaced Elliot Street, to Victoria Street, then turn up hill.

Looming large is Harrah's Sky Tower (➤ 20). Ride high to its observation decks and admire the view, or linger, if you dare, in the casino at its foot.

Walk north along Federal Street and through St Patrick's Square. Continue for one block west, then walk along Hobson Street to the water.

Ahead is the Hobson Wharf National Maritime Museum (➤ 34) and to the left the yacht basin which is to be used as the base for the America's Cup in the year 2000.

Distance
2.5km

Time
1 hour plus stops; suggest half a day

Start/end point
Queen Elizabeth II Square, at foot of Queen Street
 36B2

Lunch
Cin Cin on Quay (££)
✉ Ferry Building
☎ 09 307 6966

What to See Around Auckland

REGIONAL BOTANICAL GARDENS ⭐⭐

These extensive 64-hectare gardens out of town have been specially created for both educational and leisure purposes. A total of some 10,000 exotic and native plants found in the region are displayed and there are well laid-out walks, as well as horticultural information.

WAITAKERE CENTENNIAL DRIVE ⭐⭐

The forest-clad hills to Auckland's west offer a scenic drive with bush scenery and views around the suburbs. The drive, signposted as Scenic Route 24, commences at New Lynn and passes through Titirangi to the Arataki Park visitor centre. Here raised platforms provide excellent views of the rainforest and there are displays about its inhabitants.

A loop road goes to the peak of Pukematekeo. Other roads lead to the black volcanic sands of the beach of Piha, famous for surfing, and a gannet colony at Muriwai.

✚ 32C3
✉ Hill Road, Manurewa;
27km south of Auckland
☎ 09 303 1530 🕐 8–dusk
🍴 Café 💲 Free
♿ Good with assistance

✚ 32C3
✉ Arataki visitor centre
☎ 09 817 7134
🕐 Daily 9–5 (later closing in summer)
♿ Very good at visitor centre
💲 Free

Carvings at the Arataki visitor centre

✚ 36B3
✉ Ferry Building, Quay Street
☎ 09 367 9111
🕐 Call for cruise times
🍴 Cin Cin on Quay (££) & Harbourside restaurant at wharf
♿ Few; should be accompanied
💲 Cruise prices vary

WAITEMATA HARBOUR AND HAURAKI GULF ⭐

Waitemata Harbour, on the eastern side of the isthmus, opens on to the Hauraki Gulf. It is easily reached by frequent catamarans, fast ferries, launches and yachts from the foot of the main central street (Queen Street).

The gulf offers a number of islands to visit and opportunities for boat trips. The largest and most popular of the islands is Waiheke Island, 35 minutes away from Auckland by fast ferry. It has several craft shops and galleries as well as a number of superb beaches.

Rangitoto Island is the nearest island to the city. It is famous because the volcanic eruption that occurred here is the most recent in the region (within the last 800 years). Safari tours can be taken across the craggy rocks towards the summit.

A Drive Through Suburban Auckland

Starting from the Ferry Building, the drive heads east towards Tamaki Drive then loops inland to the suburbs of Newmarket and Remuera before returning to Quay Street.

Tamaki Drive passes the public Parnell swimming baths and Okahu Bay. Kelly Tarlton's Antarctic Encounter and Underwater World (➤ 35) is a possible stop.

Continue, taking a short side road to the Savage Memorial look-out on Bastion Point, along Tamaki Drive to Mission Bay where there is a pleasant seaside park. Follow the coast to the suburbs of Kohimarama and St Heliers.

At St Heliers' shops turn right to climb up St Heliers Bay Road. Continue to the road's end, then turn left into St Johns Road and, at the roundabout, turn right.

This road enventually becomes Remuera Road. Pass through Remuera shopping centre and then turn right into Broadway – an important artery and shopping centre for Newmarket.

From Newmarket, continue into Parnell Road.

Domain Drive on your left leads to the parklands of the Domain and Auckland Museum (➤ 34).

Return to Parnell Road and continue north to the big new Anglican cathedral on your right. Turn right here into St Stephens Avenue and left into Gladstone Road, perhaps pausing at the Rose Gardens in Gladstone Road and harbour viewpoint before dropping down to Quay Street for the return to the Ferry Building.

Distance
24km

Time
1 hour plus stops; suggest at least half a day

Start/end point
Ferry Building, Quay Street
➕ 36B3

Lunch
Saints Waterfront Brasserie (££)
✉ 425 Tamaki Drive, St Heliers
☎ 09 575 9969

Originally built as a war memorial, the Auckland Museum houses exciting displays related to the Maori culture and the natural history of New Zealand, including dinosaurs and other extinct species

39

Bay of Islands

As well as being one of New Zealand's most historically interesting regions (regarded as the cradle of European settlement), this is among the North Island's most popular resort areas. The Bay of Islands Maritime and Historic Park consists of over 800km of coastline and some 150 islands, as well as many reserves on the surrounding mainland and the communities of Paihia, Russell and Kerikeri.

Bay of Islands attracts visitors in their hundreds

➕ 32B4
✉ Kemp House and Stone Store: Kerikeri Basin, Landings Road
☎ 09 407 9236
🕐 Jun–Aug, Thu–Fri 10:30AM–12:30PM, 1:30PM–4:30PM. Closed 25 Dec & Good Fri
♿ Few; ground floor only

➕ 32B4
✉ Paihia wharf: Marsden Road

Museum of Shipwrecks
✉ Waitangi River Bridge, Te Karuwha Parade
☎ 09 402 7018
🕐 Daily 10–5
♿ None
🎟 Cheap

CAPE REINGA (➤ 17, TOP TEN)

KERIKERI ✪✪
Kerikeri, situated 23km from Paihia, is known for its citrus fruit orchards and craft workshops. It is the small harbour basin, however, that is of most interest. Historic sites here include **Kemp House**, erected in 1822 as the country's second mission station, now the oldest surviving building in New Zealand, and the **Stone Store** which was originally part of the mission settlement but is now a museum.

Across the inlet is Rewa's Maori Village, a full-size reconstruction of a pre-European Maori fishing village.

PAIHIA ✪✪
Paihia, the tourist base of the Bay of Islands, sprawls over three bays. Its town centre is the wharf, from where a variety of scenic cruises depart, as well as a regular passenger service across to Russell (➤ 41). Accommodation, restaurants and cafés are plentiful.

At the north end of Paihia, the **Museum of Shipwrecks**, housed aboard an old sailing vessel, offers genuine relics of marine history around New Zealand. The items were collected by explorer-cum-diver Kelly Tarlton, who later developed the famous underwater attraction in Auckland (➤ 35).

RUSSELL ✪✪

Russell, New Zealand's first European settlement, was known as 'the hell-hole of the Pacific' back in the days when lawless whalers came into violent contact with the local Maoris. Things have improved, however, and the town is now more of a quiet hamlet, although the bullet holes in the wooden church built in 1836 and the graves in its churchyard testify to its colourful past.

Other sights include **Pompallier House** (built for the first Catholic bishop), and nearby Flagstaff Hill – scene of disputes between British troops and local Maori in the 1840s.

The **Captain Cook Memorial Museum** includes a one-fifth scale model of Cook's ship, *Endeavour*.

WAIPOUA KAURI FOREST ✪✪

This stand of forest is a remnant of the bush which once covered nearly all the Northland region. The kauri is one of the world's largest trees, with a long straight trunk; its timber was highly prized and its gum used as a resin. The scenic road through the reserve passes many of these trees, but the largest, called 'Tane Mahuta', requires a short bush walk.

WAITANGI HISTORIC RESERVE ✪✪

Just north of Paihia is the Waitangi Historic Reserve, where, in 1840, a Treaty was signed between Maori tribes and the British Crown under the auspices of Captain (later Governor) Hobson. The Treaty promised the Maori people certain rights in exchange for British sovereignty, but its interpretation remains controversial today.

The Treaty House, built in 1833 as home for the British government representative, is open as an exhibit. The Waitangi grounds also display a centennial (1940) Maori Meeting House, and a 36-m Maori canoe.

✚ 32C4

Pompallier House
✉ The Strand
☎ 09 403 7861
🕐 Daily 10–5
✊ Moderate

Captain Cook Memorial Museum
✉ York Street
🕐 Daily 10–4
✊ Cheap

✚ 32B4
✉ SH12; 112km from Paihia
☎ 09 439 8360 (Dargaville visitor information)
🕐 Unrestricted access
✊ Free

✚ 32B4
✉ Tau Henare Drive, near Paihai
☎ 09 402 7308
🕐 Daily 9–5
🍴 Quality Resort Waitangi (££)
♿ Good if accompanied
✊ Cheap

War canoe at Waitangi

Rotorua

The city of Rotorua, 234km southeast of Auckland, is recognised as the North Island's leading tourist centre because of its geothermal activity, scenic variety and Maori culture. The volcanic activity is first apparent because of the sulphurous odours in the air.

A sheep-shearing demonstration at Rotorua Agrodome

Whakarewarewa (➤ 26) is the city's leading geothermal reserve but the area has a number of other places with such activity, plus a dozen lakes, an evergreen forest, and a host of other attractions. A selection is listed here.

The visitor information centre is in Fenton Street and the main shopping thoroughfare is Tutanekai Street.

✚ 33D1
✉ Riverdale Park, Ngongotaha
☎ 07 347 4350
🕐 Shows three-times daily. Closed 25 Dec & Good Fri
♿ Good 💰 Cheap

✚ 33D1
✉ SH30, Tikitere; 18km from Rotorua
☎ 07 345 3151
🕐 Daily 9–5
♿ Good 💰 Cheap

✚ 33D2
✉ Memorial Drive, foot of Tutanekai Street
☎ 07 348 6634 (Lakeland Queen cruise)
🕐 Two or three cruises daily
♿ Good 💰 Moderate

AGRODOME

Here the story of sheep in the New Zealand economy is told with regular displays of sheep-shearing, plus lamb feeding, mock sheep auctions and sheep and cattle shows. Several varieties of sheep are on view and tours of the farm are available. There is also a model railway display and a woollen goods shop.

HELL'S GATE 😊😊

The reserve here covers about 10 hectares and an extensive walk takes visitors past pools of hot water, bubbling mud and other features. English playwright George Bernard Shaw is supposed to have given the area its name by exclaiming, 'Hell's Gate', on first seeing it.

LAKE ROTORUA 😊

This is the largest of a dozen or so lakes in the area. The quayside area is a pleasant site where several lake cruises on different kinds of craft are available.

Mokoia Island, in the middle of the lake, is the setting for a popular Maori legend about two young lovers called Hinemoa and Tutanekai; the island can be visited.

Tudor-style St Faith's Church at the Maori village of Ohinemutu

Did you know ?

There are several places in Rotorua where concerts of Maori dance and song are performed daily. Tamaki Tours (► 113) operate an evening tour combining a concert and a hangi (► 95) in a forest setting that offers a unique Maori cultural experience.

OHINEMUTU ✪

Ohinemutu, a Maori village on the shore of Lake Rotorua, was once the lake's main settlement. It remains of interest with its Anglican St Faith's Church (notice in particular the window showing Christ dressed in a Maori cloak), and a carved Maori meeting house.

✉ Mataiwhera Street
☎ 07 348 5179 (Rotorua visitor information)
🕐 Daily 9–4:30   ♿ Few
💲 Free, or donation

RAINBOW SPRINGS ✪✪✪

Rainbow and Fairy Springs, combined as one attraction, are sites where natural freshwater gushes from the ground. There are pools of giant trout amid bush and ferns. Rainbow Farm Park, opposite Rainbow Springs, displays an array of New Zealand farm animals, including sheep and cows. There are sheep-shearing, cow-milking and sheep-dog displays; also a well-stocked souvenir shop.

✉ Rainbow & Fairy Springs: Fairy Springs Road
☎ 07 347 9301
🕐 Daily 8–5
♿ Good
💲 Moderate

SKYLINE SKYRIDE ✪✪

Mount Ngongotaha (757m) is a prominent peak on the western shore of Lake Rotorua. Although there is a road to the top, the Skyride gondola is a popular attraction, taking passengers up 200m to a viewpoint halfway up the mountain, from where there is a panorama of the city and lake. An alternative way back down is by luge (a sledge following a purpose-built track). There is a restaurant at the top of the gondola and a herb shop at its foot.

✚ 33D1
✉ Fairy Springs Road
☎ 07 347 0027
🕐 Daily 9–restaurant closing
🍴 Skyline restaurant
♿ Few
💲 Cheap

43

TE WAIROA BURIED VILLAGE ✪✪

In 1886 the previously dormant volcano of Mount Tarawera erupted, resulting in loss of life and the burying of three villages – Te Wairoa, Moura and Te Ariki – beneath several feet of lava and mud.

Also obliterated were the famous Pink and White Terraces, fan-like natural silica formations on the shores of Lake Rotomahana which had been an early tourist draw for the region. The village of Te Wairoa has since been partly excavated and may be seen separately or as part of a round trip incorporating other local sites. A small gallery displays 'before and after' pictures.

Tours of the volcano can be taken from Rotorua's visitor centre in Fenton Street.

🞤 33D1
✉ Tarawera Road; 14km from Rotorua
☎ 07 362 8287
🕐 Daily 9:30–5:30
🚌 Tour bus available
♿ Good on upper paths; waterfall track unsuitable
👍 Cheap

WAIMANGU ✪✪

Waimangu is another area with impressive volcanic activity. There is a walk past thermal pools, including a boiling 4-hectare lake, and a path leads down to Lake Rotomahana where lake cruises sail past steaming cliffs and over the sunken site of the Pink and White Terraces (► above). A round-trip tour with a small bush walk links this lake with Lake Tarawera and a return to Rotorua via Te Wairoa Buried Village (► above).

🞤 33D1
✉ Off SH5; 19km south of Rotorua
☎ 07 366 6137
🕐 Daily 8:30–5
🚌 Tour bus available
♿ Good if accompanied; site on an incline
👍 Cheap

WAIOTAPU THERMAL WONDERLAND ✪✪

The most colourful of the geothermal areas, Waiotapu features thermal zones that have been given their different hues by mineral deposits. Highlights include the Lady Knox Geyser, which plays every morning (primed with the help of soap) at 10:15 and can reach heights of 20m, and the hot Champagne Pool.

🞤 33D1
✉ Off SH5; 32km south of Rotorua
☎ 07 366 6333
🕐 Daily 9–5
🚌 Tour bus available
♿ Good **👍** Cheap

The Champagne Pool

WHAKAREWAREWA THERMAL RESERVE (►26, TOP TEN)

Taupo

The town of Taupo nestles at the heart of the North Island beside Lake Taupo, looking out towards the distant peaks of the Tongariro National Park. Together with the surrounding area, it has become a major holiday centre and offers the visitor a wealth of attractions.

HUKA FALLS ✪✪✪

Near Wairakei, where the Waikato River plunges over an 11-m drop, are the Huka Falls. Though not high, the huge volume of water that crashes through this narrow defile makes it a thunderous spectacle. There are various vantage points from the path.

🔲 33D1
✉ Off SH1; 7km north of Taupo
☎ 07 378 9000 (information)
🕐 Unrestricted access
♿ Good 💵 Free

A pleasure trip aboard the cruiser African Queen *on Lake Taupo*

LAKE TAUPO ✪

Formed thousands of years ago by a series of volcanic upheavals, Lake Taupo, covering 600sq km, is the largest lake in New Zealand.

The lake is internationally renowned for its trout fishing and fishing guides and charter boats are available. There are also cruises on the lake and along parts of the Waikato River, New Zealand's longest waterway, which flows out of the lake.

🔲 33D1
✉ Taupo visitor information: Tongariro Street
☎ 07 378 9000
🕐 Daily 8–6
🚢 Lake cruises depart from Redoubt Road
💵 Cruise prices vary

WAIPAHIHI BOTANICAL GARDENS ✪✪

This is an extensive drive-through reserve with walks lined with many species of native trees and beds of rhododendrons and azaleas. The gardens are at their best when the shrubs are in full flower during October.

🔲 33D1
✉ Shepherd Road, Taupo
☎ 07 378 2937
🕐 Open daylight hours
♿ Good 💵 Free

WAIRAKEI GEOTHERMAL POWER STATION ✪✪

The visitor centre shows how the geothermal steam is harnessed to generate electricity. Near by there is a look-out over the geothermal field.

Wairakei Thermal Valley and Craters of the Moon are other areas of geothermal activity, both featuring steaming vents and bubbling mud pools. The first has an admission fee, the second is free. Both require extensive walking.

🔲 33D1
✉ SH1; 10km north of Taupo
☎ 07 378 0254
🕐 Daily 9–4:30
🍴 Wairakei Resort
♿ Good at visitor centre
💵 Free displays

45

In the Know

If you only have a short time to visit New Zealand, or would like to get a real flavour of the country, here are some ideas:

Above and below: two aspects of traditional New Zealand life – family picnicking on the beach and a greeting Maori warrior-style

10
Ways To Be A 'Kiwi'

Love sport, follow sport, talk about sport, maybe even have a go at playing it.
Have a Sunday picnic, or an afternoon drive. Go anywhere, just go!
Go to the beach, or the bush, whenever possible.
Travel by car – everywhere. Buses are for the old and the young; trains are for tourists. Bikes… what's a bike?
Don't drink and drive. It's taken 150 years for Kiwis to learn this – some still haven't, but most people are scared of the consequences.

Don't discuss religion.
Do discuss politics. Blame everything bad on politicians.
'Shout' a Kiwi a beer. A friendly way to thank Kiwis is to 'shout' them (or buy them) a drink.
Gamble – Lotto, 'scratches', the horses, a casino, Housie, a raffle, a hunk of meat at the pub….
Don't talk between 8 and five past on a Saturday night. That's when the national Lotto is drawn.

10
Places To Have Lunch

Bell Pepper Blues (££)
 474 Princes Street, Dunedin ☎ 03 474 0973. Modern interesting selection.
Boulcott Street Bistro (££) ✉ 99 Boulcott Street, Wellington ☎ 04

499 4199. International bistro selections.

Cin Cin on Quay (££)  99 Quay Street, Auckland ☎ 09 307 6966. Busy waterfront café.

City Bistro (£££) ✉ 101 Wakefield Street, Wellington ☎ 04 801 8828. Popular American bistro dishes.

Gibbston Valley Winery (££) ✉ Queenstown–Cromwell SH6 (24km from Queenstown) ☎ 03 442 6910. Light lunches in a southern vineyard.

Iguaçu (££) ✉ 269 Parnell Road, Auckland ☎ 09 358 4804. Trendy cuisine.

one red dog (££) ✉ 151 Ponsonby Road, Auckland ☎ 09 360 1068. The best pizzas in Ponsonby.

Palazzo del Marinaio (££) ✉ Shades Arcade, City Mall, Cashel Street, Christchurch ☎ 03 365 4640. Seafood and other dishes.

Parkroyal (££) ✉ Corner Kilmore & Durham streets, Christchurch ☎ 03 365 7799. Light and elegant in this hotel atrium.

The Portage Hotel (££) ✉ Beachcomber Cruises, Picton ☎ 03 573 4309. A launch cruise and views.

10
Top Activities

Bird-watching: from November through to February take a tour to see the white heron roost near Whataroa.

Four Wheel Drive Safari: follow an old stage-coach road on the Dunstan Trail, out of Alexandra.

Bungy-jumping

Just Looking: Kelly Tarlton's Antartic Experience and Underwater World, in Auckland.

Golfing: there are over 300 courses!

Maori Experience: eat a *hangi*.

Shopping: visit St Lukes Mall in Auckland.

Skiing: try Coronet Peak, near Queenstown.

Trout Fishing: open season year-round at Taupo.

Walking: walk from the Arataki visitor centre in Auckland's Waitakere Ranges for a view of the New Zealand bush.

Wine Trail: take a tour around the Marlborough vineyards.

White-water canoeing

10
Adventure Activities

Big game fishing: Bay of Islands

Bungy-jumping: Queenstown

Canoeing: Whanganui River

Glacier walking: Fox Glacier

Hang gliding: around Queenstown

Horse riding: the old gold-mining trail out of Arrowtown

Hunting: the Kaimanawa Ranges out of Taupo

Jet-boating: Shotover River jet-boat, out of Queenstown

White-water rafting: Several places in both the North and South Islands

Wilderness walking: the Whirinaki Forest

Lower North Island

South of Lake Taupo the North Island becomes hillier. Tongariro National Park, the first of New Zealand's national parks, is dominated by a trio of volcanoes, marking the southern edge of the volcanic belt.

In the west, the city of New Plymouth is watched over by its dormant volcano, Mount Egmont. In the east, the sprawling hills of the Hawke's Bay region, a well-known wine-growing area, sweep down to the twin cities of Napier and Hastings.

Down at the southern tip of the island lies the capital city of Wellington, guarding the Cook Strait.

Within easy reach of the capital is the Wairarapa district, where the small town of Martinborough is becoming of increasing interest as a result of the boutique wineries in the area. Beyond, a road stretches down to Palliser Bay and Cape Palliser, where there are rugged, remote beaches.

'In this nasty, overcrowded and polluted world, New Zealand is as near to a people's paradise as fallible humanity is likely to get.'

AUSTIN MITCHELL
The Half-Gallon Quarter Acre Pavlova Paradise (1972)

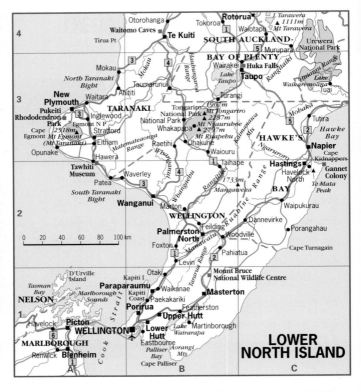

LOWER NORTH ISLAND

Wellington
European settlement commenced here in 1840 and, following its selection as New Zealand's capital in 1865, the city has never looked back.

Situated at the southern tip of the North Island, Wellington is an important commercial centre and has excellent transport links with the rest of the country – by ferry, air, rail and coach. It is also the nation's cultural centre, home town of the New Zealand Symphony Orchestra, the Royal New Zealand Ballet Company and Te Papa, Our Place, the new Museum of New Zealand. Numerous music festivals are held here each year and the entertainment scene is burgeoning.

Bounded on three sides by the sea and inland by circling hills, Wellington is a compact city, easy to get around on foot, and its fine deep harbour acts as a focal point. To provide relief from the hustle and bustle, there are plenty of gardens, parks and hilly viewpoints, as well as the nearby beaches.

It is a city with character, divided into several parts: there is the older, distinctive heart, including its Parliament and government offices; there is the sprawling Hutt Valley – largely residential, but with industry at its southern end; and there are the northern suburbs of Porirua and the long sandy beaches of the Kapiti Coast.

51

What to See in Wellington

BOTANIC GARDENS ✪✪

Spread over 25 hectares, these landscaped gardens include both native bush and exotic plants and there is also a tulip display each spring. The Lady Norwood Rose Garden with more than 100 different species of rose and a Begonia House are additional features.

At the top of the hill (near the top cable-car terminal, (► below) is the New Zealand Astronomy Centre, with a planetarium, astronomy displays and a hands-on area.

CABLE CAR ✪✪

Rising from its terminal off Lambton Quay, Wellington's main shopping street, these small historic carriages climb a 1-in-5 gradient to Kelburn. The service began in 1902, but the original wooden cable cars have been replaced. At the top, where there are fine views, is the upper entrance to the Botanic Gardens (► above), providing an alternative walking route back down (► 53).

KATHERINE MANSFIELD BIRTHPLACE ✪

New Zealand's greatest short-story writer was born in this wooden house in 1888. Now restored and furnished appropriately for the period, the building is open for viewing and has permament and changing exhibitions. The garden has been laid out in its original Victorian design.

MARITIME MUSEUM ✪✪

Displays featuring the history of Wellington harbour, over 80 model ships, sea-going paraphernalia and old photos, plus lots more, illustrate the long maritime associations of the region. The museum is housed in the old Harbour Board building (1891) on Queens Wharf.

✚ 50B1
✉ Tinakori Road, Glenmore Street & Upland Road
☎ 04 801 3071
🕓 Unrestricted access
🚠 Cable car
♿ Few; slopes and steps in parts
🎟 Free

✚ 50B1
✉ Cable Car Lane, off Lambton Quay
☎ 04 801 7000 (Ridewell timetable enquiries)
🕓 7AM (Sat & Sun 9AM)–10
♿ None; assistance required
🎟 Cheap

The birthplace of renowned author Katherine Mansfield

✚ 50B1
✉ 25 Tinakori Road
☎ 04 473 7268
🕓 Tue–Sun 10–4
♿ Few; assistance required
🎟 Cheap

✚ 50B1
✉ Jervois Quay
☎ 04 472 8904
🕓 Mon–Fri 9:30–4, Sat–Sun & hols 1–4:30
♿ Few 🎟 Cheap

A Walk Around Wellington

An extra dimension is given to this walk by first of all taking a ride on the cable car (➤ 52) from its terminus in Cable Car Lane, off Lambton Quay, up past the university to the Kelburn terminus. This will require the purchase of a one-way ticket. From here on it's all downhill.

After alighting from the cable car, go to the look-out points to admire the city and harbour views.

Immediately adjacent is the upper entrance to the Botanic Gardens (➤ 52). Follow any of the paths downhill through the gardens.

At the bottom, continue around Anderson Park then go through Bolton Street Memorial Park, carry on over the motorway and then go down the steps to Bowen Street.

Stroll through the grounds of Parliament, passing the Beehive, the Parliament House and the Parliamentary Library buildings. Exit onto Molesworth Street and cross over to the National Library, which contains the Alexander Turnbull Collection (➤ 54).

Continue walking up Molesworth Street, then turn right into Pipitea Street to reach Mulgrave Street.

Here you can take the opportunity to visit Old St Paul's Church (➤ 54) and admire its interior design and decoration.

Carry on along Mulgrave Street to the Railway Station and Lambton Quay. Take a leisurely stroll along this busy shopping street, perhaps visiting the Kirkcaldie & Stains department store, before returning to Cable Car Lane.

Distance
2.5km walk

Time
1.5 hours plus stops

Start/end point
Cable Car Lane, off Lambton Quay
🚇 50B1

Lunch
Café at the National Library (£)
✉ 58–78 Molesworth Street
☎ 04 474 3000
🕐 Mon–Fri 9:30–4

Colourful, formal flowerbeds in the Botanic Garden

NATIONAL LIBRARY AND NATIONAL ARCHIVES

This modern building facing the cathedral contains reference copies of books and periodicals retained throughout New Zealand's history.

An important part is the famous Turnbull Collection of 55,000 historic New Zealand and worldwide publications, bequeathed on Turnbull's death in 1918. Included are a number of rare first editions, including perhaps the world's finest collection of work by John Milton, English poet.

Close by are the **National Archives**, where special papers and treasures relevant to New Zealand history are stored and displayed. Included among a number of historical documents is the 1840 Treaty of Waitangi, and a 1776 letter of instructions to Captain James Cook.

OLD ST PAUL'S CHURCH ✪✪

The 'old' church dating from 1866, so-called to distinguish it from the new 1972 cathedral, is now used for concerts rather than prayer. However, its fine colonial Gothic style and its history have secured it as a property of the Historic Places Trust, so safe-guarding its future.

PARLIAMENT BUILDINGS ✪✪✪

The most distinctive of the Parliament Buildings complex in downtown Wellington is the Beehive, designed by Sir Basil Spence and erected in 1982. It houses ministerial offices and the Cabinet Room. Next to it is the Parliament House – New Zealand's one chamber parliament and the adjacent building is the Parliamentary Library. Near by are Government Buildings, the world's second largest wooden building, built in 1876, which now houses the Victoria University of Wellington Law Faculty.

TE PAPA, OUR PLACE, MUSEUM OF NEW ZEALAND ✪✪✪

Now housed in a huge new $280 million contemporary edifice on the waterfront, the collection consists of hundreds of national treasures portraying the story of New Zealand and its peoples (its full Maori name, Te Papa Tongarewa, means 'Repository of Things Precious'). The building also houses the National Art Gallery.

What to See Around Wellington

DAYS BAY AND EASTBOURNE ✪

Although these village suburbs, nestling on hilly slopes on the eastern shores of Wellington's harbour, are connected to the city by road and ferry, they feel worlds away. The two beaches are 15 minutes' walk apart. Behind Eastbourne village, with its cafés, craft and antique shops, the Butterfly Creek track is a favoured local tramp, while Williams Park, behind Days Bay, is popular for picnicking.

🕂 50B1
🕐 Up to eight sailings per day
🍴 Blue Penguin café at Days Bay
🚌 81, 83 via Petone
⛴ Trust Bank Ferry from Queens Wharf

DOWSE ART MUSEUM ✪✪

Situated at Lower Hutt in the Hutt Valley, to the north of Wellington, this is an established local collection of contemporary New Zealand art, glassware and artefacts from local Maori culture.

From time to time various special local and touring exhibitions are mounted, for which an entry fee is charged.

🕂 50B1
✉ 45 Laings Road, Lower Hutt
☎ 04 570 6500
🕐 Mon–Fri 10–4, Sat–Sun & hols 11–5
🍴 Café on premises
🚌 83 via Petone
🚂 Hutt Central, then buses to Lower Hutt
🖐 Free

Left: *Modern Civic Square is the location for Wellington's Information Centre*

FELL ENGINE MUSEUM ✪✪

Beyond the city, the Wairarapa district offers a variety of rural attractions. The Fell Engine at Featherston is a special steam locomotive that was used on the railway built over the Rimutaka ranges, before the tunnel was made.

The Rimutaka Incline walkway (☎ 04 564 8551 – DoC Rimutaka Forest Park information centre) follows the route of the former line from the edge of the Wellington conurbation. Totalling 18km, the walk takes between four and five hours to complete.

🕂 50B1
✉ Fell Engine Museum: Corner Lyon & Fitzherbert streets, Featherston
☎ 06 308 9780
🕐 Sat 10–4; Sun 1 (10AM in summer)–4
♿ Good
🖐 Cheap

Did you know ?

The Chatham Islands, an isolated group of islands 850km east of Wellington, will be the first to welcome the new millennium. Their local time is actually 45 minutes ahead of another close contender, Gisborne, New Zealand's most easterly city and one of the closest to the International Date Line.

Opposite: *the rich interior of Old St Paul's Church, constructed exclusively with native timber*

🚆 50B1

🚉 Plimmerton, Paekakaruki
or Paraparaumu (☎ 04
498 3000) then buses 1,
2, 3 or 4

❓ Shopping mall opposite
station at Paraparaumu

**Southward Vintage Car
Museum**

✉ Otaihanga Road,
Waikanae; 55km north of
Wellington

☎ 04 297 1221

🕐 Daily 9–4:40

🚌 Tour buses

♿ Good

💰 Cheap

*A copper car, one
of the more
unusual exhibits
in the Southward
Vintage Car
Museum*

KAPITI COAST ⭐⭐

Consisting of the dormitory suburbs of Paekakariki and
Paraparaumu to the north of Wellington, the Kapiti Coast is
known for its fine white sandy beaches and good watersports facilities. Kapiti Island, 5km offshore, is a bird
sanctuary with restricted access. Boat trips depart from
Paraparaumu.

Southward Vintage Car Museum, located beyond
Paraparaumu, is one of the largest private collections of
vintage automobiles and other forms of transport found
anywhere.

🚆 50B1

☎ Freely accessible

🚌 20; also tour buses

MOUNT VICTORIA LOOK-OUT ⭐⭐⭐

Rising from Wellington's inner suburbs, this 196m peak
offers a splendid (but usually windy) view of the
surrounding city and harbour. It is thought to have been
used as a look-out point by the Maori: their name for it
means 'to watch the sky'. Several narrow winding roads
provide access.

🚆 50B1

✉ Wilton Road, Wilton; 20
minutes from the city
centre

☎ 04 475 3245

🕐 Open all hours

🚌 14 Wilton

♿ Outdoor paths

OTARI NATIVE BOTANIC GARDEN ⭐

New Zealand's largest collection of indigenous plants is
cultivated and displayed here in 80 hectares of parkland
and 2 hectares of cultivated gardens. Habitats include
native bush, natural forest, an alpine garden and a fernery.
The profusion of birdlife that thrives in the park undisturbed is an added bonus.

There are over 8km of walking tracks, graded according
to length, several picnic areas and an information centre.

A Drive Around Wellington

Wellington's Marine Drive commences on Oriental Parade, near the eastern end of Courtenay Place. Note the many narrow and one-way streets in the city centre.

Once on Oriental Parade, continue round Oriental Bay past Mount Victoria (➤ 56).

To drive up Mount Victoria, take Majoribanks Road opposite Courtenay Place then follow signs along narrow climbing streets to the Admiral Byrd Memorial and Lookout.

Follow Oriental Parade around the point into Evans Bay, passing boating facilities and slipways. Turn left on to Cobham Drive, passing the northern end of the airport runway, then keep left out to the next point.

Shelly Bay Road follows the other side of Evans Bay to Point Halswell. Note the Massey Memorial to former Prime Minister William Ferguson Massey (1856–1925).

The route continues down past Scorching, Karaka and Worser Bays. Continue through Seatoun and Pass of Branda to rejoin the coast.

Breaker Bay Road follows a bleak stretch of coastline at the harbour entrance. Off-shore is Barrett Reef, the craggy rocks where the *Wanganella* ran aground in 1947 and the *Wahine* foundered in 1968. Moa Point Road leads back to the southern end of the airport runway. Keep on going round Lyall Bay to Island Bay for more views out across Cook Strait.

Return to the city either via Happy Valley and Ohiro and Brooklyn roads to Willis Street and Lambton Quay, or via The Parade and Adelaide Road back to Cambridge Terrace and Courtenay Place.

Distance
40km

Time
2½ hours

Start/end point
Courtenay Place
✛ 50B1

Lunch
Zino's Restaurant (££)
✉ 351 The Parade, Island Bay
☎ 03 383 8256
🕐 Lunch Sun–Fri, dinner nightly

Lambton Harbour

Napier

Hawke's Bay is the name given to the hinterland of hills sweeping down towards the central east coast. At the foot of the hills are fertile plains – 'the fruit bowl of New Zealand' – and the twin cities, just 20km apart, of Napier and Hastings. Both were casualties of a tragic earthquake in 1931.

The rebuilding of Napier in the contemporary architecture of the time has made its art deco design an attraction and the traffic-free malls in the centre of the town create a pleasant shopping environment.

Typical art deco architecture in Napier

➕ 50C2
✉ Cape Kidnappers reserve; access by tour only
☎ 06 834 4161 visitor information
♿ None
🖐 Tours moderate; book locally

➕ 50C2
Hawke's Bay Museum
☎ 06 835 7781
🕐 Tue–Fri 10–4:30, Sat–Sun 1–5
♿ Good

Kiwi House
☎ 06 834 1336

Marineland
☎ 06 835 7599
🕐 Daily 10–4:30
♿ Few

Aquarium
☎ 06 835 7579
🕐 Daily 9–5
♿ Few

➕ 50C2
✉ Te Mata Peak Road; 31km south of Napier
🕐 Top part of road closes at sunset

CAPE KIDNAPPERS ✪✪
The world's largest known mainland colony of Australasian gannets lies 32km southwest of Napier at the southernmost tip of Hawke Bay. These large seabirds arrive in July and lay their eggs in October and November, hatching about six weeks later. The best time to visit the reserve is between October and April.

MARINE PARADE ✪✪✪
Attractions along the esplanade include **Hawke's Bay Museum** which has an audio-visual section devoted to the 1931 earthquake plus other interesting displays including one devoted to eastern Maori culture and another to art deco from around the world; and the **Kiwi House**, where you can discover all you want to know about kiwis. Here these shy nocturnal birds are kept in natural surroundings and can be seen feeding. At **Marineland**, seals, sealions, penguins and dolphins can all be seen, some partaking in performing shows. Swimming with the dolphins is another option. Finally, for those interested in underwater life, there is the **Aquarium**. A huge fish tank housing several different species forms the centrepiece of the aquarium where sharks, turtles, crocodiles, plus a number of other animals, are resident. Divers brave enough can even join the inmates of the giant fish tank.

TE MATA PEAK ✪✪
A narrow road climbs via Havelock North right to the top of this 399m viewpoint offering a spectacular panorama over the Heretaunga Plains to the Hawke's Bay region.
The peak forms part of the 98-hectare Te Mata Park, which has several good walking routes.

TONGARIRO NATIONAL PARK (▶ 23, TOP TEN)

New Plymouth

With the development of oil and gas reserves in the region, the city of New Plymouth in northern Taranaki has become an 'energy capital', but it is also well known for its parks and gardens (it is sometimes dubbed the Garden City) and as the hub of a prosperous dairying region. This in part is due to the fertile deposits from Mount Egmont (Taranaki), a landmark for miles around.

MOUNT EGMONT/MOUNT TARANAKI

Visible from parts of New Plymouth and most of Taranaki, Mount Egmont, also known as Mount Taranaki, rises 2,518m up from the coastal plain. It was named by Captain Cook (after the Earl of Egmont, who had been First Lord of the Admiralty prior to Cook's departure) after sighting it in 1770. Weather conditions can be unpredictable on the mountain, but this does not deter the numerous climbers attracted by it.

The surrounding 33,000-hectare Egmont National Park has a small winter ski-field and several walking tracks.

50A3
Visitor centre on Egmont Road
06 756 8710
Open access
Free

Lush greenery in Pukekura Park

PUKEITI RHODODENDRON PARK

A Trust operates these gardens featuring brilliant displays of rhododendrons and azaleas amidst 360 hectares of native bushland. The best time to visit is September to November, and in late October the city promotes these and other gardens as part of a Rhododendron Week.

50A3
Upper Carrington Road; 29km from New Plymouth
06 752 4141
Daylight hours daily
Few Cheap

PUKEKURA PARK

Chief among many parks in the city, these gardens have fountains, a fernery, woodland and two lakes as features.

Adjoining, but separated by a concert bowl, is the more formal Brooklands Park where there is a rhododendron dell, European-style flower gardens, as well as sporting grounds.

50A3
Liardet Street
06 759 6080 (New Plymouth visitor information)
Both gardens free
Few

Upper South Island

Although one-third larger in area than the North Island, the South Island has only one-quarter of the country's population. What it lacks in demographics, however, it more than makes up for with its variety of scenery.

Several national parks lie in the northern half of the South Island, from the bush and beach scenery of Abel Tasman National Park on the north coast to the great glaciers of Westland on the west coast, a place of legend where men have searched for jade, gold, coal and timber. In between, the Southern Alps and their foothills offer alpine vistas and a host of opportunities for walking and the study of wildlife.

Christchurch is the South Island's main international gateway and its largest city. Considered the most 'English' of New Zealand's cities, it stands on the edge of the Canterbury Plains.

‘ The great drawback to New Zealand comes from the feeling that after crossing the world and journeying over so many thousand miles, you have not at all succeeded in getting away from England. ’

ANTHONY TROLLOPE
Australia and New Zealand
(1873)

UPPER SOUTH ISLAND

5

4

Cape Foulwind
Westport
Charleston 6

Paparoa
National Park
Punakaiki
**Pancake Rocks
& Blowholes**

Grey

3

Greymouth
Shantytown

Lake
Brunner

Hokitika
Lake
Mahinapua

Lake Otira
Kaniere

Ross

Arthur's Pass
2400m
Mt Murchison

WESTLAND

White Heron Sanctuary Harihari

Whataroa 6

2795m
Mt Arrowsmith

Lake
Coleridg

2

Franz Josef
Gillespies Point Franz Josef Glacier
Fox Glacier Fox

Mount Cook
National Park

Arrowsmith Range

Mount Hutt

Westland 3498m
National Mt Tasman
Park Mt Cook 3754m
Tasman Glacier

2545m
The Thumbs

Methven

Rangitata

3157m Mount
Cook

Lake
Tekapo

Plains Village

Haast

Southern Alps

Ben Ohau Range

Lake Tekapo

Canterbury

Landsborough

Two Thumb Range

Opihi

Jackson Head Jackson
Bay
Cascade Point

Mount Aspiring
National Park

Haast Pass

Hunter

Lake
Obau

Mackenzie
Country

Fairlie

The Hunters Hills

Temuka
Pleasant Point

1

3027m
Mount
Aspiring

Dart

Olivine Range

Young Range

Lake
Wanaka

Ahuriri

Twizel

Lake
Pukaki

Kirkliston Range

Timaru Caroline
Bay

Lake
McKerrow

Rees

Shotover

Treble Cone
2088m 6

Lake
Hawea

8

Omarama

Lake
Benmore

Lake
Aviemore

1

Hollyford

Clutha

Otematata

Wanaka

A

B

Waimate

C

62

Cape Farewell
Farewell Spit
Collingwood
Golden Bay
Kahurangi Point
1213m
Mt Stevens Takaka
Totaranui
Cape Stephens
D'Urville Island
Kapiti I
Kahurangi National Park
Abel Tasman National Park
Marlborough Sounds
Paraparaumu
Kaiteriteri
Pelorus Sd
Oparara
Motueka
Tasman Bay
Porirua
Upper Hutt
Karamea
Keneperu Sd
Queen Charlotte Sd
Karamea Bight
Nelson
Richmond
Havelock
Picton
Arapawa
WELLINGTON
Lower Hutt
Motupiko
Brightwater
Cloudy Bay
Turakirae Head
Granity
Mt Owen 1875m
Wairau
Renwick
Blenheim
Denniston
Richmond Range
MARLBOROUGH
Buller Gorge
Rotoroa
St Arnaud
Seddon
uller
Murchison
Lake Rotoiti
Waihopai
Awatere
Cape Campbell
Victoria Forest Park
Lake Rotoroa
Nelson Lakes National Park
Inland Kaikoura Range
efton
Spenser Mts
Clarence
Seaward Kaikoura Range
Lewis Pass
Kaikoura
Whale Watching Tours
Kaikoura Peninsula
1834m Mt Ajax
Hanmer Forest Park
Hanmer Springs
Lake Summer
1612m Mt Tekoa
Waiau
rthur's Pass ational Park
Culverden
Hurunui
Cheviot
1987m Mt Crossley
Porter Heights
Puketeraki Range
Ashley
Rangiora
Pegasus Bay
RBURY
Kaiapoi
Antarctic Centre
rana Park Wildlife Trust
Waimakariri
Christchurch
Darfield
Heathcote
Air Force World
Ferrymead
Lyttelton
Rakaia
Historic Park
Lake Ellesmere
Banks Peninsula
Ashburton
nwald
Akaroa
Akaroa Harbour
ains
Canterbury Bight

0   20   40   60   80   100 km

D   E   F

Christchurch

Founded as a Church of England colony in 1850, much of the charm of Christchurch rests with those colonial beginnings, the graceful lines of some of its early Gothic stone buildings contrasting with those of more contemporary design. The city is named after England's Oxford University college, where the city's founding father was educated.

Much of interest lies in the compact downtown area, with the willow-lined Avon River, complete with ducks and ornate bridges, winding around its cathedral and lively central square. Beyond the city centre numerous parks and gardens grace the flat suburbs, giving Christchurch the epithet (like many another New Zealand town) of Garden City. To the south, the Port Hills separate the city from its port at Lyttelton on Banks Peninsula and New Zealand's only French settlement, Akaroa.

As the hub of the South Island's air, rail, and road services, the city also makes a good touring base. Many coach trips start and finish here, with options such as whale-watching at Kaikoura, swimming at Hanmer, taking a train through the Alps, skiing in winter, or even visiting Mount Cook, New Zealand's highest mountain, within a day's touring.

Students punting on the river in Christchurch in time-honoured tradition

What to See in Christchurch

ARTS CENTRE ⭐⭐
Alive with stalls, live entertainment and food stalls at weekends, this graceful complex, once part of the university, is equally charming on weekdays. Shops, workshops and galleries sell and display arts and craft works, making it a good place to look for souvenir items and gifts at any time, and there are several cafés, restaurants and bars on the premises. The professional Court Theatre group performs here regularly.

☩ 66A1
✉ Worcester Boulevard
☎ 03 366 0989
🕐 Daily 10–4:30
🍴 Food stalls on premises
🚊 Tourist tramway
♿ Few; assistance suggested
🎟 Free

AVON RIVER ⭐⭐
This stream adds a restful charm to the city centre as it meanders through Christchurch and there are pleasant riverside walks alongside. Various boats can be hired – including punts: enquire at the visitor centre.

The Town Hall is a modern (1972) complex consisting of an auditorium, a theatre, meeting rooms and a restaurant which overlooks the river.

☩ 66A1
✉ Visitor centre, Corner Worcester Boulevard & Oxford Terrace
☎ 03 379 9629
🕐 Mon–Fri 8:30–5; visitor centre Sat–Sun 8:30-4

BOTANIC GARDENS ⭐⭐
The 30-hectare Botanic Gardens lie within Hagley Park, a vast recreation area on the fringe of the central business district where all kinds of organised sports take place. Set amid the wooded lawns are a number of themed gardens (rose, rock, azalea) and there are many displays of flowering trees and exotic plants. Glasshouses specialise in orchids, ferns and tropical plants, among others.

☩ 66A1
✉ Rolleston Avenue
☎ 03 366 1701
🕐 Gardens: daily 7AM–1 hour before sunset; conservatories: 10–4:15
🍴 Restaurant & café
🚊 Christchurch tramway
♿ Few

CANTERBURY MUSEUM ⭐⭐⭐
This is a general collection relating to New Zealand history and ethnology, with two specialist exhibits of particular interest, namely the Moa Hunters, life-size dioramas of early Maori and the giant flightless bird – now extinct, and the Hall of Antarctic Discovery, with relics from the Scott expedition, and others.

☩ 66A1
✉ Rolleston Avenue
☎ 03 366 8379
🕐 Daily 9–5 (later in summer)
🍴 Coffee shop at museum
🚊 Tourist tramway
♿ Good
🎟 By donation

65

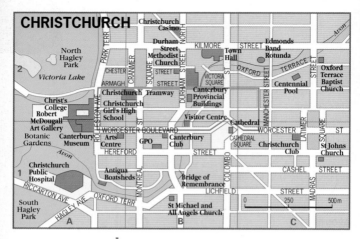

CHRISTCHURCH

🏛 66B2
✉ Corner Durham & Armagh streets
☎ 03 366 1100
🕐 Mon–Sat 10:30–3; Oct–May Sun 2–4
🚃 Tourist tramway
♿ Few; assistance required
💲 Free

CANTERBURY PROVINCIAL BUILDINGS ✪✪

Built in 1858 beside the Avon River, this neo-Gothic-style complex reflects the city's English heritage and the early days of local government when there were 13 independent provinces in New Zealand. These were the main government buildings for the Canterbury province. Of special interest is the 1865 Council Chamber, with stained-glass windows and a vaulted ceiling.

Christchurch Casino, one of only two in New Zealand

🏛 66B2
✉ Victoria Street
☎ 03 365 9999
🕐 Mon–Wed 11AM–3AM; Thu 11AM–Mon 3AM continuously
♿ Good
❓ Dress code prohibits jeans

CHRISTCHURCH CASINO ✪

There are two levels of action in this casino filled with gambling machines and tables. Its European style contrasts with Auckland's Las Vegas-style emporium at the base of Harrah's Sky Tower (➤ 20).

CHRISTCHURCH CATHEDRAL ✪✪
The building of this Gothic-style edifice, crowned with a 65-m copper-clad spire, was begun in 1864 at the heart of the original Church of England settlement. The cathedral was completed 40 years later. There are 133 steep stone steps up to the top of the bell tower, but, as might be expected, the views from the top are worth the effort.

CHRISTCHURCH TRAMWAY ✪✪
Electric trams first came to Christchurch in 1905 but the network was closed down in the early 1950s. Now, restored vintage trams take tourists on a newly created scenic route through the city, taking in many of the best sites and shopping areas. Full-day passes are available and passengers can hop on and off to suit.

> ### Did you know ?
> One of the enduring sights in Cathedral Square is a figure dressed in black robes and a wizard's hat who makes it his business to mock both the preachers and the visitors who gather round. He holds forth at about 1PM on most days.

ROBERT MCDOUGALL ART GALLERY
Situated behind the Canterbury Museum (➤ 65), with access via the Botanic Gardens, the gallery exhibits New Zealand and British paintings, as well as a whole range of other works of art, including ceramics and photography.

✚ 66B1
✉ Cathedral Square
☎ 03 366 0046
🕐 Opens 8:30AM; tower closed till 11:30AM Sun
🚋 Christchurch Tramway
♿ Good ✋ By donation

✚ 66B2
✉ From Cathedral Square
☎ 03 366 7830
🕐 Continuous service daily
♿ Difficult access
✋ Cheap

Above: *the Christchurch Tramway is a good way of seeing the city's sights*

✚ 66A1
✉ Botanic Gardens
☎ 03 366 8379
🕐 Daily 10–5:30 (winter 4:30)
🍴 Coffee shop at Canterbury Museum
🚋 Tourist tramway
♿ Good ✋ By donation

Many boat trips around the bays of the Banks Peninsula leave from Akaroa Harbour

What to See Around Christchurch

AIR FORCE WORLD

The Royal New Zealand Air Force Museum, at the former air base at Wigram in Christchurch's western suburbs, reflects the history of military aviation in New Zealand from the earliest days. As well as the aircraft and related displays, authenticated with figures and scenery, there are several hands-on exhibits.

AKAROA AND BANKS PENINSULA

Within days of the British declaring sovereignty over New Zealand in 1840, a shipload of French settlers founded Akaroa on the Banks Peninsula to the southeast of Christchurch and it has remained French in spirit.

The mountainous Banks Peninsula is a large volcanic outcrop, with the original craters now forming Lyttelton and Akaroa harbours (➤ 70, 71). Allow time for a cruise.

CHRISTCHURCH GONDOLA

Ride up the side of Mount Cavendish by aerial cable-way from the terminal near the Lyttelton tunnel entrance at Heathcote for a great view over Christchurch and Lyttelton. There is a restaurant, a kiosk, a shop and a Time Tunnel display (admission extra) at the upper terminal.

FERRYMEAD HISTORIC PARK

This is a living museum of transport and technology with a working tramway, railway and village, plus displays about household appliances, wirelesses, fire engines and aviation, amongst others. Hundreds of mechanical musical instruments are another feature. Several volunteer groups are responsible for different portions of the park.

HANMER SPRINGS

Formerly an alpine spa, this outdoor recreation centre 135km north of Christchurch offers skiing in winter and adventure options such as jet-boat rides and bungy jumping. The prime attraction, however, is the Thermal Reserve with its hot pools set in landscaped grounds.

63D2
Main South Road, Wigram
03 343 9532
Daily 10–5. Closed 25 Dec
Café on premises
8, 25 Good
Cheap

63E2
SH75; 83km from Christchurch
03 379 9629 (Christchurch visitor centre)
Several restaurants, especially French
Day tours available

63D2
Bridle Path Road
03 384 4914
Daily 10AM–evening
Restaurant at summit
28 None Cheap

63D2
269 Bridle Path Road, Heathcote
03 384 1970
Daily 10–4:30. Closed 25 Dec
3 Good Cheap

63D3
Pools: Amuri Road
03 315 7128 Daily. Closed 25 Dec Café
Good Cheap

A Walk Around Christchurch

Start at Cathedral Square, taking a look at the cathedral itself (➤ 67).

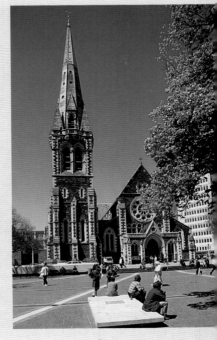

Stroll due west along Worcester Street to the Avon River (➤ 65). The Bridge of Remembrance to the left was built to commemorate Kiwi troops who died during World War I. The visitor information centre is on the right before you cross the river: punting can be organised here.

Worcester Street continues as a renovated boulevard. After crossing Montreal Street, pause at the Arts Centre (➤ 65). At weekends, when there are outdoor stalls as well as the many shops, allow extra time.

Next the Canterbury Museum (➤ 65) looms in front. Behind the museum, the Robert McDougall Art Gallery (➤ 67) is worth taking a look at.

Continue for two blocks north on Rolleston Avenue, passing Christ's College, and turn east into Armagh Street. Pass Cranmer Square.

At the Durham Street intersection, note the grand architecture of the Canterbury Provincial Buildings (➤ 66).

Cross the Avon again to enter Victoria Square. Across the square, past statues and fountains, note the the Town Hall.

Colombo Street leads back to Cathedral Square, where there is usually something of interest – buskers, preachers, performers – taking place.

Much of the route is followed by the Christchurch Tramway (➤ 67) so, if in doubt, follow the tracks – or take a ride.

Christchurch Cathedral Square, where there is nearly always something to watch

Distance
2.5km

Time
1½ hours plus stops

Start/end point
Cathedral Square
✚ 66B1

Lunch
Annie's Wine Bar and Restaurant (££)
✉ Arts Centre, 2 Worcester Boulevard
☎ 03 365 0566

Hands-on at the Centre

- 🚩 63D2
- ✉ Orchard Road, Harewood
- ☎ 03 358 9896
- 🕐 Daily 9:30–5:30 (8PM summer). Closed 25 Dec
- 🍴 Café 🚌 Airport bus
- ♿ Good 💲 Cheap

- 🚩 63D2
- ✉ SH74; 13km from Christchurch
- ☎ 03 379 9629 (Christchurch visitor information)
- 🕐 Harbour launch to Diamond Harbour 11:15 & 2:45
- 🚌 28

- 🚩 63D2
- ✉ McLeans Island Road, Harewood
- ☎ 03 359 7109
- 🕐 Daily 10–4:30. Closed 25 Dec
- 🍴 Restaurant
- 🚌 Phone re transport
- ♿ Few 💲 Cheap

70

INTERNATIONAL ANTARCTIC CENTRE   ✪✪✪

Located next to the airport, and the Operation 'Deep Freeze' base of the United States Air Force, this modern facility displays the geography and science of the southern polar regions with exhibits and wide-screen movies. Highlights include a walk-through ice cave and an Antarctic aquarium. There is also an interesting souvenir shop and an interactive room.

LYTTELTON   ✪

Christchurch's port is accessible via a 2-km road tunnel, as well as by the hilly roads over the Port Hills.

In addition to the attraction of the harbour and its associated boat trips, the Lyttelton Museum, which includes an Antarctic section, and the Time-ball Station, where ships could once determine noon by the sighting of a falling ball signal, are of interest.

ORANA PARK WILDLIFE TRUST   ✪

Animals from Africa, Australia, Asia and the Americas can be seen in this 80-hectare wildlife park, New Zealand's largest, which specialises in breeding endangered and rare species. There is also a farmyard featuring domestic animals, a reptile house, native bird aviaries and a nocturnal kiwi house, plus lots more.

TRANZALPINE TRAIN (► 24, TOP TEN)

A Drive to Akaroa & Banks Peninsula

From Christchurch, the route heads east out to the Banks Peninsula; there are alternative options for the return.

From Cathedral Square, drive south along Colombo Street. After several blocks, turn west (to the right) on to Moorhouse Avenue and follow signs to the left for Akaroa, leading to SH75.

The route leaving the city leads across flat country to Birdlings Flat, skirting Lake Ellesmere, a shallow wetland separated from the sea by the gravelly Kaitorete Spit.

Turn inland to Little River, a former railway terminus.

From here the road climbs steeply up to Hilltop for views over Akaroa Harbour, the crater of an extinct volcano.

The road then drops steeply and follows the harbour round to Akaroa (➤ 68), 83km from Christchurch.

Akaroa's Gallic ancestry is clearly visible in street names and architecture. In addition to local walks, gardens, a museum and an historic lighthouse, a worthwhile attraction is a cruise around the harbour. The *Canterbury Cat* operates daily at 1:30PM for 2 hours, often sighting Hector's dolphins, penguins and seals.

There are alternative return routes to Christchurch, including the high narrow Summit Road. Either follow the ridge around to Hilltop, or cross over to follow a hilly route round to Lyttelton harbour. From there, choose the tunnel, the Dyers Pass route to Christchurch, or take the Evans Pass route on to Sumner beach and then continue your journey to Christchurch.

Distance
166km

Time
Allow a full day

Start/end point
Cathedral Square
➕ 66B1

Lunch
L'Hotel Wine Bar & Café (££)
✉ 75 Beach Road, Akaroa
☎ 03 304 7559

View across Akaroa Harbour, one of the most attractive areas of the Banks Peninsula

What to See in Upper South Island

ABEL TASMAN NATIONAL PARK (► 16, TOP TEN)

BLENHEIM   ✪✪

At the top of the South Island, the Marlborough district is New Zealand's sunniest region and as a result the countryside around the town of Blenheim is the premier wine-making area. Marlborough sauvignon blanc is especially renowned and local wine-tasting tours are available from Blenheim and Picton.

Central Blenheim has a pleasant shopping area and several attractive gardens. **Brayshaw Historic Museum Park** includes old farming equipment, a mock colonial village and children's attractions.

FOX AND FRANZ JOSEF GLACIERS   ✪✪✪

These two huge glaciers, some 25km apart, are the main features of Westland National Park. Both are unique in that they descend as low as 300m in temperate zones.

Guided tours and hikes, including helicopter trips, are available from the villages of Fox and Franz Joseph where there are visitor centres: the headquarters of the national park, which includes a display about the glaciers, is at Franz Josef.

HAAST   ✪✪

Situated 117km south of Fox Glacier (► above), this tiny settlement marks the entrance to the Haast Pass route through the Southern Alps to Wanaka and Queenstown.

Now designated a World Heritage Area by Unesco, the Haast region includes New Zealand's most extensive area of wetlands, rain forests, coastal lagoons and swamps. Displays at the visitor centre relate to the abundant wildlife of the area and its early inhabitants.

KAHURANGI NATIONAL PARK   ✪✪

Formerly known as Northwest Nelson Forest Park, this is the second largest national park in New Zealand. Largely mountainous with very few roads through it, the park is well known for its Heaphy Track, a 77-km long walking route. Forest and bush-clad countryside covers the

Sidebar (left column):

✚ 63E4
Brayshaw Historic Museum Park
✉ New Renwick Road
☎ 03 578 1712
🕐 Mon–Sat 10–4; Sun 1:30–4
▥ Cheap

✚ 62B2
✉ Glaciers: SH6; 187km from Greymouth

Franz Josef Visitor Information
☎ 03 752 0796
🕐 Summer 8:30–7; winter 8:30–12, 1–4:30

✚ 62A1
✉ SH6; 345km southwest of Greymouth
☎ 03 750 0809 (Haast visitor information)
🕐 Daily 8:30–4
🚌 Daily from the glaciers & Queenstown

✚ 63D5
✉ Via SH60 toCollingwood; 136km from Nelson
☎ 03 525 9136
🕐 Open access to park
🚌 Shuttle transfers arranged locally
▥ Free access

marble and limestone karst country which is riddled with extensive cave systems, the vast majority of which are closed to the public.

KAIKOURA ✪✪
This small seaside town on the rocky Kaikoura Coast was formerly a whaling station and has become popular as a whale-watching centre with trips available year round.

The main road north and south of the town offers splendid coastal scenery, and the local Maori Leap Cave (3km out) is known for its limestone formations.

☩ 63E3
✉ SH1; 191km north of Christchurch
☎ 03 319 5641 (Kaikoura visitor information)
🚌 From Christchurch, Blenheim & Picton daily

LAKE TEKAPO ✪✪
Accessible from the main road between Christchurch and Mount Cook village, the lake lies at the northern end of the barren Mackenzie Country basin. Glacial deposits account for the turquoise colour of the water.

A picturesque small stone chapel situated on the edge of the lake, built to commemorate the pioneer farmers of the area, is a favourite tourist stop. Alpine flights are also available from here.

☩ 62C2
✉ SH8; 226km west of Christchurch
🍴 Restaurants available
🚌 Daily from Christchurch & Queenstown

MOUNT COOK NATIONAL PARK (➤ 21, TOP TEN)

Whale-watching off the Kaikoura Coast

63E4
SH6; 438km north of Christchurch

Suter Art Gallery
Bridge Street
03 548 4699
10:30–4

NELSON

Surrounded and sheltered by hill's, the sunny city of Nelson is the main commercial centre of a rich fruit-growing region. Above all, however, it is noted for its arts and crafts, pottery in particular because of the availability of good local clay, and this is displayed at several venues around the town. Foremost among these is the **Suter Art Gallery**, which has local exhibitions as well as a permanent collection.

Paths in the Botanical Reserve lead up to a viewpoint reputed to be the 'centre' of New Zealand.

63D3
Via SH6 & SH63; 119km south of Nelson
03 521 1806
Free access to park
Daily bus from Nelson

NELSON LAKES NATIONAL PARK

Inland, south of Nelson, the tiny village of St Arnaud is the main gateway to this mountainous reserve best known for its twin lakes of Rotoroa and Rotoiti. St Arnaud stands on the shores of the latter and is the main centre for boating, fishing and picnicking. Apart from lake access, there are no roads within the park.

63E4/F5
SH1; 28km north of Blenheim
03 573 7477 (Picton visitor information)
From Wellington
Portage Hotel on luncheon cruise (10:15–4:30)

Marlborough Sound

PICTON AND MARLBOROUGH SOUNDS

Picton, at the head of Queen Charlotte Sound, is the commercial centre for the sea inlets formed from the drowned valleys collectively known as the Marlborough Sounds. It is also the South Island port for the inter-island ferry service from Wellington.

Moored up on the waterfront is the hulk of the 1853 clipper ship *Edwin Fox* – a former carrier of tea, troops, convicts, meat and coal; it is currently being restored. Picton Museum has a varied local collection, including whaling relics.

Various launch cruises can be taken around the sounds and there are also a number of walking routes, some requiring several days to complete, with a selection of lodge accommodation along the way.

Taking a breather to admire the view of Lake Pukaki, with Mount Cook in the background

Did you know ?

The last stronghold of the black stilt, the world's rarest wading bird, is among the rivers threading through the Mackenzie Basin. Once common in New Zealand, numbers have dwindled to less than 100 due to loss of their breeding habitat. A captive breeding programme has been established at the Black Stilt Aviary just outside the town of Twizel.

TWIZEL AND LAKE PUKAKI ✪✪

The road from Twizel to Mount Cook village (➤ 21) runs alongside the glacier-fed Lake Pukaki, known for its distinctive blue colouring. At 16sq km, it is the South Island's fifth largest lake.

Originally built as a servicing town for the giant Upper Waitaki hydro-electricity scheme, Twizel has survived to service the tourist industry and local rural scene.

WESTLAND NATIONAL PARK (➤ 72, FOX AND FRANZ JOSEPH GLACIERS)

WHITE HERON SANCTUARY ✪

Amid the lagoons that lie on the northern fringes of Westland National Park, beside the Waitangi-roto River, lies New Zealand's only breeding site for the white heron. Between November and February, when they are nesting, these majestic birds can be seen on tours leaving from Whataroa which include a jet-boat ride, a ride in a mini-van and a short walk.

🔲 62B1
✉ SH8; 284km southwest of Christchurch
☎ 03 435 0802 (Twizel Field & information centre)
🍴 Cafés & hotel restaurant
🚌 Daily from Christchurch & Queenstown

🔲 62B2
✉ SH6; 154km south of Greymouth
☎ 03 753 4120
🕐 Access controlled
🚌 Daily from Nelson, Greymouth & the glaciers
♿ Not good 💰 Expensive

Food & Drink

As a nation, New Zealanders like to eat and drink well and visitors will find no shortage of good places to eat. As well as authentic New Zealand food, often served in restaurants displaying a 'Taste New Zealand' sign, there are many ethnic restaurants to choose from, offering a variety of dishes.

Above: *informality is the keynote of New Zealand restaurants*
Above right: *opening up a Maori* hangi

The international fast-food chains are well represented and take-away establishments are common. Shopping malls often have a food hall and these are especially well patronised at lunchtime.

Meat

Lamb is the traditional meat of New Zeland, usually served roasted with mint sauce or jelly, but beef, pork and chicken are all widely available. Canterbury lamb is particularly well thought of. Hogget is one-year-old (the tenderest) lamb.

Individual meat pies, filled with either steak, mince, or chicken, sometimes with gravy, cheese or potato as well, are widespread and popular.

Seafood

A number of seafood delicacies are available throughout the country either as starters or main courses. These include Nelson scallops, Marlborough mussels, Bluff (deep sea) oysters from the far south of the South Island and west coast whitebait. Seafood soups, especially chowders, are also popular.

Fish dishes are widespread, often featuring snapper, orange roughy, *terakihi*, groper (*hapuka*), flounder, blue cod and John Dory. Salmon are reared in the south but trout, although a popular game-fish, is not caught commercially, nor offered in restaurants.

Fruit and Vegetables

A wide variety of locally grown vegetables is available, including potatoes, peas, beans, pumpkin, lettuce, carrots and corn. *Kumara* is a native sweet potato. Seasonal fresh fruit, grown locally, includes apples, peaches, pears and plums.

The prickly skinned kiwifruit (bright green inside) was known as Chinese gooseberry until the Kiwis decided to market them as their own. Now they are branded as Zespri.

Desserts

Steamed and baked puddings abound in winter, but fresh fruit and creamy New Zealand ice-cream is a year-round favourite: hokey-pokey, a kind of butterscotch flavour, is particularly popular. But the dessert New Zealand claims as its own (although Australians refute that) is pavlova – a meringue base covered with a layer of whipped cream and topped with fresh kiwifruit or strawberries.

Kiwifruit, just one of the many fruits that thrive in New Zealand's fertile soil and temperate climate

Drink

New Zealand's tap water is perfectly safe to drink and fresh milk and cream are plentiful.

Generally, New Zealanders are a nation of beer drinkers and a variety of draught beers and lagers are brewed in the country.

Home-produced wine is gaining an increasingly recognised reputation internationally; Chardonnays in particular are widely acclaimed.

Mealtimes

Kiwis usually have a light breakfast and lunch and a substantial evening meal. Dinner and 'tea' usually refer to the evening meal – eaten between 6 and 8PM. Supper is usually an evening coffee before bed. Morning and afternoon tea breaks (smokos) – 10 minutes at 10AM and 3PM – are essential.

Most motels offer self-catering facilities, but will provide a cooked breakfast on request. Hotel prices rarely include breakfast.

Lower South Island

Fiordland, one of the world's largest and most spectacular national parks, covers the far southwest corner of the South Island, its shoreline slashed by great inlets stretching far inland into a region of forests and lakes. Gateway to the area is the resort of Te Anau, situated on the shore of its great lake.

Lovers of the great outdoors are attracted to the bustling city of Queenstown, on Lake Wakatipu. Within easy reach of fiords, skiing and adventure options of many kinds, it is an international resort of world fame. South is Invercargill, regional capital of Southland and the main departure point for New Zealand's often forgotten third island, Stewart Island, well off the main tourist track and a haven for bush wildlife.

The main commercial centre of the region, however, is Dunedin, sometimes dubbed 'the Edinburgh of the South'.

' The danger is that, when people find out what an interesting place New Zealand is they may come in crowds. ... I strongly advise you not to make too much of the tourist sights except for yourselves. '

GEORGE BERNARD SHAW
What I Said in New Zealand (1934)
published in the *Auckland Star* (1934)

Queenstown

New Zealand's second largest lake, Z-shaped Lake Wakatipu, with the Remarkables mountain range serving as a backdrop, provides a dramatic setting for the town of Queenstown nestling snugly on its northeastern shore.

This is undoubtedly New Zealand's premier resort for adventure and action, offering a whole host of exhilarating activities ranging from jet-boating up and down the nearby Shotover and Kawarau rivers to helicopter trips over the mountains, from bungy-jumping to skiing at Coronet Peak, from parachute jumps to white-water rafting.

Less sensational but equally appealing are the gentler pursuits of lake cruising on an old steamboat, walking, back-packing and fishing. For those who prefer just to look, there are a number of places to visit (museums, parks and gardens) in and around the town. Not to be missed is the Skyline Gondola (► 22) for spectacular views of the lake.

The nightlife here is just as lively, with many bars, cafés and restaurants to choose from and a whole range of entertainment lasting long into the night. Shoppers, too, are well catered for, with the pedestrianised streets of the Mall and Church Street running down to the waterfront, the colourful focal point of the town.

Formerly a gold-mining town, Queenstown has relied on tourism since the beginning of this century and now leaves no stone unturned in its efforts to attract visitors from around the world.

Lake Wakatipu, together with the surrounding mountains, is responsible for Queenstown's development as an outdoor-activities resort

The TSS Earnslaw *steamer making a visit to Walter Peak Farm on the lakeshore*

What to See In Queenstown

TSS *EARNSLAW* ★★

The lake steamer TSS *Earnslaw*, built in 1912, operates frequent cruises from its wharf near downtown. This 'lady of the lake' offers local sightseeing trips and excursions to Walter Peak Farm, a high-country sheep station across the lake where sheep-shearing and dog-handling are demonstrated.

KIWI AND BIRDLIFE PARK ★

A number of avaries, including some housing endangered species, a native bush area and a nocturnal kiwi house are the main attractions here. Ponds and landscaping provide an attractive, natural setting.

QUEENSTOWN GARDENS ★

Queenstown Gardens, with trees and shrubs, flower gardens and recreational areas, cover a small promontory jutting into the lake. They were established in 1867. There are views through the trees of the mountains from the short walk along the beach from downtown.

Williams Cottage, at the entrance to the gardens, is one of Queenstown's oldest buildings.

QUEENSTOWN MOTOR MUSEUM ★

A collection of vintage cars, motorcycles and aircraft, plus an assortment of motoring memorabilia, make up this museum next to the Skyline Gondola terminal. Special exhibitions change on a regular basis.

QUEENSTOWN'S SKYLINE GONDOLA (➤ 22, TOP TEN)

UNDERWATER WORLD AQUARIUM ★

An underground observatory with huge windows, situated at the end of the main pier on Queenstown Wharf, allows spectators to view at close quarters the lake's wildlife, such as trout and eels, swimming around.

Sidebar listings:

✚ 82C4
✉ Steamer Wharf
☎ 03 442 7500
◷ Departs regularly
🍴 Evening cruise offers dinner at Walter Peak
♿ Few 👊 Moderate

✚ 82C4
✉ Brecon Street
☎ 03 442 8059
◷ Daily 9–5

✚ 82C4
✉ Marine Parade or Park Street
☎ 03 442 4100 (Queenstown visitor information)
◷ Unrestricted access
♿ Few

✚ 82C4
✉ Brecon Street
☎ 03 442 8775
◷ Daily 9–5:30

✚ 82C4
✉ Rees Street
☎ 03 442 8437 ◷ 9–5
♿ None 👊 Cheap

A Walk Around Queenstown

The first part of this stroll around Queenstown is flat, but the second part involves a climb in the countryside.

From the wharf at the foot of the main mall, outside Eichardts Tavern, walk towards the peninsula jutting out into the lake. This short stroll, either along the lake's beach or adjacent footpath, leads to the Queenstown Gardens (➤ 80).

Here paths lead through flowers and trees, as well as past recreational amenities such as tennis courts and a bowling rink. There are views back through the trees to downtown Queenstown or out over the lake. The southeastward view across the lake incorporates the Remarkables range.

The Botanical Gardens in Queenstown, occupying a small promontory jutting into the lake

Loop around to the access road (Park Street) and walk up the streets behind Queenstown. Turn left at the top of Sydney Street into Hallenstein Street, then right into Edgar and Kent streets.

From here note the signposted Queenstown Hill Walkway. Follow this path for some 4.5km, rising to a height of about 850m. The path alternates through bush (mostly exotic trees, including pine and fir), with the vegetation becoming scrubbier at higher altitudes. There are patches of schist rock and a small tarn on the way.

The view opens out over the town, the lake and surrounding mountains to reveal the steep glaciated valleys and mountainsides of the district.

After viewing the spectacle, return by the same route.

Distance
10km

Time
3½ hours

Start/end point
Foot of The Mall
✚ 82C4

Lunch
A drink & 'counter lunch' at Eichardts Tavern (£)
✉ The Mall, Queenstown
☎ 03 442 8369

LOWER SOUTH ISLAND

5

Jackson Head *Jackson Bay*
Cascade Point
Mount Aspirin
National Par
Awarua Point
Big Bay
Martins Bay Lake McKerrow
Olivine Range
3027m Mount Aspiring
Yates Point
Milford Sound
Darran
Dart
Rees
Richardson
2088
Trebl Co
1692m
Milford Sound
Mitre Peak Homer Tunnel
2819m
Bligh Sound
George Sound
Franklin Mts
Milford Track
Kinloch
Glenorchy
Arrowtow
Humboldt
Coronet Peak
Skippers Canyon
Queenstown
Frankt
Caswell Sound
Stuart Mts
Glade House

4

Charles Sound
Fiordland
Murchison Mts
Te Ana-au Caves
Livingstone Mts
Skyline Gondola
Lake Wakatipu
Secretary I
Doubtful Sound
Thompson Sound
Kepler Mts
Lake Te Anau
Eglinton Valley
Kingston
The Remarkables
Dagg Sound
National Park
West Arm
Te Anau
Kepler Track
Mararoa
Eyre Mts
6

3

Breaksea Sound
Wilmot Pass
West Arm Underground Powerhouse
Lake Manapouri
Manapouri
Hunter Mts
Resolution Island
Dusky Sound
L Monowai
Kakapo Mts
Takitimu Mts
Mossburn
S O U T H L A N D
Lumsden
West Cape
Cameron Mts
Watau
Aparima
Oreti
Riversdale
Chalky Inlet
Lake Poteriteri
Lake Hauroko
Otautau
Winton
Gore
Mataura
Puysegur Point
Te Waewae Bay
Tuatapere
6
Mataura

2

Pahia Point
Riverton
Invercargill
1
Solander I
Centre
Bluff
Stirling Point
Bluff Harbour
Toetoes Bay
Waipap Point
F o v e a u x
Codfish I
980m
Mount Anglem
Halfmoon Bay (Oban)
Ruapuke Island
S t r a i t
Mason Bay
Paterson Inlet
750m
Mt Allen

1

Stewart Island
South West Cape

A | B | C

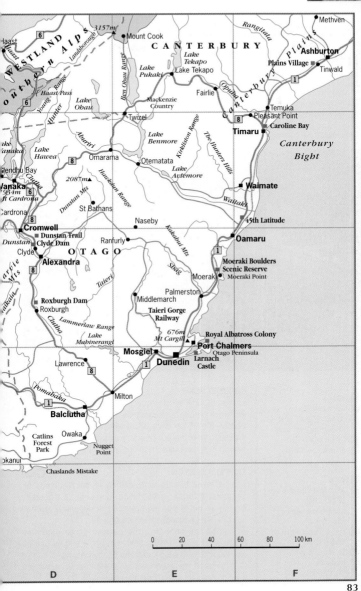

Methven

Rangitata

CANTERBURY

Mount Cook
3157m

Landsborough

WESTLAND

Southern Alps

Haast

Ben Ohau Range

Lake
Tekapo
Lake Tekapo

Canterbury Plains

Ashburton
Plains Village
Tinwald

1

6

Haast Pass

Young Range

6

Hunter

Lake
Ohau

Mackenzie
Country

Fairlie

Opihi

Temuka
Pleasant Point

8

Timaru
Caroline Bay

Twizel

Lake
Pukaki

Ahuriri

Lake
Benmore

Kirkliston Range

The Hunters Hills

Canterbury
Bight

Lake
Hawea

8

Omarama

Otematata

Lake
Aviemore

Waimate

Lake
anaka

Clutha

Glendhu Bay

934m
Mt Cardrona

6

2087m

Dunstan Mts

St Bathans

Naseby

Waitaki

45th Latitude

Cardrona

Hawkdun Range

8

Cromwell

Dunstan

Dunstan Trail
Clyde Dam

O T A G O

Ranfurly

Kakanui Mts

Oamaru

1

Clyde

Taieri

Moeraki Boulders
Scenic Reserve
Moeraki Point

8

Alexandra

Manrie Mts

Shag

Moeraki

Waikaia

Roxburgh Dam
Roxburgh

Lammerlaw Range

Palmerston

Middlemarch

Clutha

Lake
Mahinerangi

Taieri Gorge
Railway

676m
Mt Cargill

Royal Albatross Colony

Port Chalmers

Lawrence

8

Mosgiel

1

Dunedin
Larnach
Castle

Otago Peninsula

Pomahaka

Milton

1

Balclutha

Catlins
Forest
Park

Owaka

Nugget
Point

okanui

Chaslands Mistake

0   20   40   60   80   100 km

D   E   F

What to see Around Queenstown

ARROWTOWN

With its stone cottages and non-indigenous trees such as sycamore and oak, the old gold-mining town has a great deal of charm. The main shopping street in particular is delightful to stroll along, and a visit to the Lakes District Centennial Museum is well worthwhile.

The return trip to Queenstown via Lake Hayes is especially beautiful in the autumn.

🕂 82C4
✉ 20km from Queenstown
☎ 03 442 4100 (visitor information)
🍴 Restaurants & cafés
🚌 Local shuttle service

Old-fashioned Arrowtown

CORONET PEAK

Between June and October this is one of the region's leading ski-fields, but it is worth visiting at any time of the year as the 15-km drive offers sky-high views over Lake Wakatipu and the surrounding countryside. During the season a regular bus service operates to the field.

🕂 82C4
✉ 15km from Queenstown
☎ 03 442 4620 (Coronet Peak visitor information)
🍴 Winter only
🚌 Shuttle in ski season

SKIPPERS CANYON

The narrow cliff-side road leading to the remnants of Skippers, a former gold-mining township, is the main attraction here, but experienced drivers only (rental vehicles are excluded) should attempt it.

The bridge spanning the narrow gorge over the Shotover River upstream, near the road's end, is one of two Queenstown sites known for bungy-jumping.

A gorge in the lower section of the river is known for the Shotover Jet speed-boat thrill ride.

🕂 82C4
✉ 28km from Queenstown
☎ 03 442 4100 (Queenstown visitor information)
🕐 Half-day tours depart 8:45AM & 2PM
🚌 Small tour buses
🏃 Moderate

A Drive from Queenstown to Milford Sound

Whether taken by rental car or coach tour, the most popular excursion from Queenstown is the round trip to Milford Sound (➤ 18). Allowing time for a cruise on the fiord, it is a 12-hour day.

From Queenstown drive 6km round to Frankton on SH6A to join SH6, southbound.

The road winds around the bluffs above Lake Wakatipu, passing Kingston at its southern end before rising over a crest to enter farmland.

The main road leads to Lumsden to pick up SH94 west, but follow the signposted short cut via Five Rivers.

From Mossburn, the road crosses progressively more barren countryside. Note a loop road to Manapouri before arriving at Te Anau (➤ 90).

From Te Anau, SH94 turns northwards, then runs parallel with Lake Te Anau and enters the beech-tree forest of the Eglinton Valley. As the mountains close in, the Divide is crossed into the upper Hollyford Valley and the road climbs up to the Homer Tunnel. On emerging from this, the road zig-zags down to Milford Sound where a hotel and an air-strip have been built. The road terminates here and return is via the same route, although tours offer coach/fly options.

A cruise on the fiord, with its high steep sides and big waterfalls, is certainly recommended. The facilities at Milford are limited, but there is basic accommodation and catering available.

In winter the road is prone to snow and possible avalanches.

Distance
291km each way

Time
A 12-hour day with stops

Start/end point
Downtown Queenstown
✚ 82C4

Lunch
Meals available on Milford Sound cruise boats

Cruise ships are dwarfed by the grandeur of Milford Sound

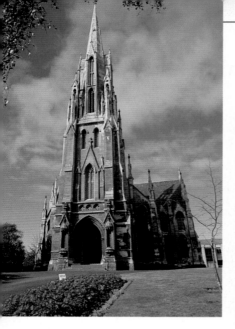

Dunedin

The town was founded in 1848 by settlers of the Free Church of Scotland at the head of Otago Harbour, a long waterway sheltered by the scenic Otago Peninusla (➤ 89). Prosperity soon followed in the wake of the 1860s Otago goldrush and the city became New Zealand's wealthiest, leaving a legacy of handsome, well-preserved buildings. Above all Dunedin is a university city (New Zealand's first university was founded here in 1869), with a lively social and arts scene.

Dunedin's First Church, a Presbyterian Gothic-style church built between 1868 and 1873

The Octagon, at the centre of the town, is dominated by a statue to the Scottish poet Robbie Burns and the imposing Anglican St Paul's Cathedral. The fact that the country's only whisky distillery is located in Dunedin is another reminder of its Scottish connections.

Extensive formal gardens (the first to be created in New Zealand) at the northern end of the city include a rose walk, the Ellen Terry garden, a rhododendron dell (best seen between October and November when the shrubs are in bloom), azalea beds and winter gardens.

HOCKEN LIBRARY ✪

Part of the university, the library (founded by Dr T M Hocken, 1836–1910) houses a collection of historic books, early manuscripts, paintings and photographs relating to New Zealand and the Pacific. More material about the nearby Otago region in particular has recently been added. General browsing of shelves is not permitted.

✚ 83E2
✉ Main site, Hocken Building
☎ 03 479 1100
🕐 Mon–Fri 9:30–5, also Tue 6–9; Sat 9–noon
♿ Good ❓ Due to move in 1998 to corner Anzac Avenue & Parry Street

OLVESTON ✪✪

This handsome stone Jacobean-style house, built at the beginning of the 20th century, illustrates the lifestyle of its wealthy owners, the Theomin family. Most of the well-preserved contents of the house, including a collection of paintings, were collected during the family's extensive travels overseas.

✚ 83E2
✉ 42 Royal Terrace
☎ 03 477 3320
🕐 Set tours daily: 9:30, 10:45, 12, 1:30, 2:45 & 4PM
♿ None 🎟 Cheap

Multi-coloured portal outside the Otago Settlers Museum

OTAGO MUSEUM ✪
Noted particularly for its Maori and Pacific Island sections, the museum, founded in 1868, also has a good natural history section, a maritime exhibition and several decorative arts items from Asia. The Discovery World section, with many scientific hands-on exhibits, brings the museum up to date.

🗒 83E2
✉ 419 Great King Street
☎ 03 477 2372
🕐 Mon–Fri 10–5, Sat & Sun 12–5
♿ Few; assistance required
✋ Free

OTAGO SETTLERS MUSEUM ✪✪
Recently considerably revamped and expanded into the Railways Bus station next door, the museum tells the story of the region's history and includes a gallery hung with photos of early settlers of the region, manuscripts and displays of their relics – there are even two steam locomotives.

🗒 83E2
✉ 31 Queens Gardens
☎ 03 477 5052
🕐 Mon–Fri (Sat 10)–4:30, Sun 1:30–4:30
♿ Assistance suggested
✋ Moderate

SIGNAL HILL ✪✪
Located in suburban Opoho, this 393-m peak offers a fine view over central Dunedin. A viewing terrace erected in 1940 marks the centennial of the British pioneers in New Zealand.

🗒 83E2
✉ End of Signal Hill Road
☎ 03 474 3300 (Dunedin visitor information)
🕐 Unrestricted ♿ Few

TAIERI GORGE RAILWAY ✪✪
The four-hour return trip along the craggy Taieri Gorge aboard a diesel-hauled excursion train leaves Dunedin Station most afternoons. As well as the scenery, there are many Victorian bridges and viaducts to admire.

Dunedin Station, a grand Edwardian building with an ornate interior, is worth seeing for itself.

🗒 83E2
✉ Dunedin Railway Station
☎ 03 477 4449
🕐 Departs 1:30 winter; 2:30 summer
🍴 Refreshments on train
♿ Few ✋ Moderate

What to See in Lower South Island

BLUFF ⭐
Invercargill's port of Bluff, 27km away from the town, lies under Bluff Hill at the tip of the South Island. A road leads up to a look-out with views across the harbour to Stewart Island (► 90). Highway One goes to land's end at Stirling Point, with its much photographed signpost indicating distances to Cape Reinga, London and elsewhere.

82C2
SH1; 27km south of Invercargill
03 218 9753 (Invercargill visitor information)

CATLINS ⭐⭐
This coastal strip at the southeast corner of the South Island has a spectacular coastline of rugged, lonely beaches, while inland lie tracts of undisturbed forests where there is a wealth of flora and fauna.

83D2
138km east of Invercargill
03 415 8371 information

CROMWELL ⭐⭐
Located east of Queenstown, in the barren landscape of Central Otago, Cromwell was partly rebuilt in the 1980s when the Clutha River was dammed to form Lake Dunstan. The story of the Clyde Dam, and Cromwell's origins as a gold-mining settlement, is presented in the town's information centre and museum.

83D3
SH6; 57km from Wanaka
03 445 0212 (Cromwell visitor information)
Scheduled coach service daily from Christchurch, Queenstown & Dunedin

FIORDLAND NATIONAL PARK (► 18, TOP TEN)

INVERCARGILL ⭐
New Zealand's southernmost city, Invercargill lies in a flat pastoral region close to the Foveaux Strait. Its main attraction is the **Southland Museum and Art Gallery** in Queens Park, a complex featuring displays about natural history, colonial settlers and the Maori heritage. Two important attractions are an enclosure displaying New Zealand's rare lizard-like tuatara reptile and a presentation about the wildlife of the sub-Antarctic islands – five uninhabited rocky clusters lying up to 700km to the south.

82C2
Southland Museum and Art Gallery
Gala Street
03 218 9753
Mon–Fri 9–5, Sat–Sun 10–5
Good
Free or donation

LAKE MANAPOURI AND DOUBTFUL SOUND ⭐⭐⭐
The best way to enjoy the beauty of this large lake is by taking a cruise. The most popular trip is to West Arm where an underground hydro-electric power scheme has been built. Access to the powerhouse is by coach along a 2-km tunnel. Some tours continue across the Wilmot Pass to the remote sea inlet of Doubtful Sound, where another cruise can be taken.

82B3/A3
12km south of Te Anau
03 249 6602
Cruises depart 9:30 summer, 9:45 winter for sound; also 1:30 summer for West Arm only
Not good
West Arm: moderate; Doubtful Sound: expensive

MILFORD SOUND (► 18, TOP TEN)

MILFORD TRACK ✪✪
Often described as 'the finest walk in the world', this 119-km track runs between the top of Lake Te Anau to Milford Sound. Boat access is required at both ends, and walkers can choose either to travel independently, over-nighting in park huts, or join a fully guided trip. Both options require advance bookings.

➕ 82B4
☎ 03 249 8514 for bookings

OTAGO PENINSULA ✪✪
The craggy peninsula guarding Dunedin's harbour is renowned for it variety of wildlife, but also has a number of man-made attractions. Among these is Larnach Castle, built in 1871, complete with ballroom and battlement. Following a chequered history, the castle has been renovated and is open to view. There is limited accommodation. Glenfalloch Gardens are also popular.

There are several wildlife reserves on the peninsula, but the most special is the **Royal Albatross Centre** at Taiaroa Head, the world's only mainland colony for giant royal albatrosses. This natural colony has a special viewing gallery and there is also an interesting visitor centre.

➕ 83E2
Royal Albatross Centre
✉ Harrington Point Road
☎ 03 478 0499 (booking essential)
🕐 10AM–dusk (from 9AM in summer)
🍴 Cafeteria at Centre
♿ Visitor centre good; viewing observatory not good
Moderate
❓ Viewing observatory closed Sep–mid-Nov

Did you know ?
The eggs laid by the giant royal albatross in November hatch roughly 11 weeks later, with each parent taking turns to incubate them. The chicks remain at Taiaroa until the following September when they take their first flight. Adult birds range over 2,000km of sea, returning to breed in alternate years. They have wingspans of up to 3m.

The royal albatross, ungainly and awkward on land but a superb flier; it sometimes stays in the air for days on end

Above: a number of trips and outdoor activities in Fiordland start from Lake Te Anau

STEWART ISLAND

New Zealand's third island, covering 1,746sq km, lies 27km south of the South Island. It can be reached by air from Invercargill or by catamaran from Bluff. Largely undeveloped, the rugged island is known mainly for fishing, and for its bush-walks and birdlife. There are few roads, but several walking tracks and a selection of accommodation.

TE ANAU

Gateway to the Fiordland National Park (➤ 18), the township beside Lake Te Anau is the main tourist town for the district and the start point for a number of walking tracks and boat cruises.

One of the latter takes visitors across the lake to the **Te Ana-au Caves**, where an attraction is a glow-worm grotto, the insects' sticky threads lighting the roof of a cave like twinkling stars.

In Te Anau, as well as the National Park Visitor Centre, where there is historical and practical information about all aspects of the park, the Wildlife Centre is of interest. Here the takahe (*Notornis mantelli*), a flightless bird once thought to be extinct, is exhibited.

WAITOMO CAVES (➤ 25, TOP TEN)

WANAKA

Situated at the eastern entrance of the Haast Pass to South Westland, Wanaka stands on the shores of Lake Wanaka, at 193sq km the South Island's third largest lake. The town is a smaller, quieter version of Queenstown, and although lacking the international pizazz that its neighbour enjoys, has just as much to offer in terms of outdoor thrills, with skiing at the Treble Cone, Cardrona and Waiorau ski-fields (in season). It is also the headquarters of and gateway to the **Mount Aspiring National Park**, a remote wilderness stretch of the Southern Alps centred around Mount Aspiring, a peak of 3,033m.

Where To...

Upper North Island

Prices

Prices, inclusive of goods and services tax (▶ 104), are approximate. They are based on a three-course meal for one without drinks and service:

£ = under $25
££ = $25–50
£££ = over $50

Auckland

Antoine's Restaurant (£££)

Renowned up-market New Zealand food cooked in modern French manner.

✉ 333 Parnell Road ☎ 09 379 8756 🕐 Lunch weekdays, dinner & supper Mon–Sat. Closed Sun

Le Brie (££)

French Provincial-style restaurant in city centre.

✉ 8 Chancery Street ☎ 09 373 3935 🕐 Lunch Mon–Fri, dinner Mon–Sat

Cin Cin on Quay (££)

Popular café in downtown Ferry Building.

✉ 99 Quay Street ☎ 09 307 6966 🕐 Mon–Fri 11AM–1AM, Sat–Sun 8AM–1AM

Frasers Place (££)

Delicatessen and light meals with eastern Europe influence.

✉ 116 Parnell Road, Parnell ☎ 09 377 4080 🕐 Lunch Mon–Sat

Iguaçu (££)

Popular, informal brasserie in Parnell.

✉ 269 Parnell Road ☎ 09 358 4804 🕐 Lunch & dinner daily; also brunch weekends

Kelly's Café (£)

Light meals at the harbour edge, adjacent to the Kelly Tarlton Underwater World attraction.

✉ 23 Tamaki Drive, Orakei ☎ 09 528 5267 🕐 Daily 10am–4pm 🚌 Any 72- to 76-

The Loaded Hog (£)

Lively tavern serving light meals. Their own beers are brewed on the premises.

🕐 104 Quay Street ☎ 09 366 6491 🕐 Daily 11AM–10PM

New Orient (££)

Chinese restaurant in central city.

✉ Strand Arcade, 233 Queen Street ☎ 09 379 7793 🕐 Lunch & dinner daily

one red dog (£)

Busy pizza café in older but trendy inner city suburb.

✉ 151 Ponsonby Road ☎ 09 360 1068 🕐 Lunch to late daily

Sails Restaurant (£££)

Popular restaurant with views of harbour bridge.

✉ Westhaven Marina; 2km from downtown ☎ 09 378 9890 🕐 Lunch & dinner daily

Saints Waterfront Brasserie (££)

Suburban restaurant with harbour views.

✉ 425 Tamaki Drive, St Heliers ☎ 575 9969 🕐 Lunch & dinner daily, also brunch Sat–Sun from 10AM

Tony's Lord Nelson Restaurant (££)

Busy city-centre steak house.

✉ 37 Victoria Street ☎ 09 379 4564 🕐 Lunch Mon–Fri, dinner Mon–Sat

Top of the Town (£££)

Award winning restaurant at top of Hyatt Regency Hotel. Good views, high prices.

✉ Waterloo Quadrant ☎ 09 366 1234 🕐 Lunch Mon–Fri, dinner Mon–Sat

Wings (££)

Restaurant and bar overlooking popular suburban beach.

✉ 71 Tamaki Drive, Mission Bay ☎ 09 528 5419 🕐 Lunch & dinner daily; open from 10:30AM Sun

Bay of Islands

Ferryman's Restaurant (££)
Seafood in a nautical location; 4km from Paihia.
✉ **Opua Store Building, 3 Beechy Street, Opua wharf** ☎ **09 402 7515** ⏲ **Daily 10AM–10PM**

The Gables Restaurant (££)
Seafood and other meals in a vintage building.
✉ **The Strand, Russell** ☎ **09 403 7618** ⏲ **Dinner daily in summer, Jun–Sep, Wed–Sun**

Quality Resort Waitangi (££)
Quality eating in a pleasant location.
✉ **Tau Henare Drive, Waitangi** ☎ **09 402 7411** ⏲ **Dinner daily; snacks at other times**

Tides Restaurant (££)
Seafood specialties in an interesting setting.
✉ **Williams Road, Paihia** ☎ **09 402 7557** ⏲ **Dinner daily in summer, Mon–Sat in winter**

Rotorua

Aorangi Peak (£££)
A 'Taste New Zealand' winner with mountain-top views.
✉ **Mountain Road, Mount Ngongotaha, on Rotorua's outskirts** ☎ **07 347 0046** ⏲ **Daily lunch & dinner**

Chapmans Restaurant (££)
Excellent New Zealand buffet.
✉ **THC Rotorua Hotel, Froude Street, Whakarewarewa** ☎ **07 348 1189** ⏲ **Lunch & dinner daily**

Incas Café (££)
Standard cuisine in a colourful setting.
✉ **Corner Fenton & Pukaki streets** ☎ **07 348 3831** ⏲ **Dinner only**

Lewisham's (££)
European-style cuisine in Rotorua's main street.
✉ **115 Tutanekai Street** ☎ **07 348 1786** ⏲ **Lunch Mon–Fri, daily dinner. Closed Tue dinner**

Orchid Garden Café (££)
Light meals, including breakfast, amid flowers and gardens.
✉ **Hinemaru Street** ☎ **07 347 6182** ⏲ **Daily**

Rumours (££)
Award-winning restaurant with local and imported foods.
✉ **81 Pukuatua Street** ☎ **07 347 7277** ⏲ **Dinner Tue–Sat**

Street Café (££)
Light trendy cuisine; outdoor option at Prince's Gate Hotel.
✉ **1 Arawa Street** ☎ **07 34 81179** ⏲ **Dinner only**

Taupo

Cobb & Co Restaurant (£)
Good value family dining.
✉ **Corner Tongariro & Tuwharetoa Streets, Taupo** ☎ **07 378 6165** ⏲ **Lunch & dinner daily**

Edgewater Restaurant (£££)
Right on the lake at Manuels Hotel, 2km from town centre. Imaginative New Zealand dishes.
✉ **Lake Terrace, Taupo** ☎ **07 378 5110** ⏲ **Dinner only**

Nonni's (££)
Popular café and restaurant in central Taupo.
✉ **Corner Lakefront & Tongariro Street** ☎ **07 378 6894** ⏲ **Daily 7AM–late**

Licensing Laws
A licensed restaurant is able to sell wine, beer or spirits with a meal. A BYO (bring your own) license means that customers can take in their own wine, although they may be charged for corkage, including use of glasses: some places are both licensed and BYO. Wine bars and licensed cafés are becoming more common throughout the country.

Lower North Island

Alcohol and the Law
The legal drinking age for imbibing in bars and taverns is 20, although 18- and 19-year-olds may drink in a restaurant in the company of someone aged 20 or over. Bars are open daily, all day, until 11pm or later.

Remember that roadside tests for alcohol and blood samples may be taken at random from any driver of a vehicle.

Wellington

Boulcott Street Bistro (£)
Light interesting bistro food in lively surroundings.
✉ 99 Boulcott Street ☎ 04 499 4199 🕐 Lunch Mon–Fri, dinner Mon–Sat

Bengal Tiger (££)
Long-established and popular Indian restaurant with a good-value evening buffet.
✉ Level 2, the Majestic Centre ☎ 04 472 8706 🕐 Lunch Mon–Fri, dinner daily

Brasserie Flipp (££)
Contemporary brasserie with contemporary food.
✉ 103 Ghuznee Street ☎ 04 385 9493 🕐 Lunch & dinner daily

Burbury's (£££)
Up-market cuisine at the top of the Plaza International Hotel.
✉ 148 Wakefield Street ☎ 04 473 3900 🕐 Dinner Tue–Sat

City Bistro (££)
Busy bar and café with New Zealand and American food.
✉ Civic Square, 101 Wakefield Street ☎ 04 801 8828 🕐 Lunch & dinner daily

Cobb & Co Restaurant (£)
Family dining in suburban Hutt Valley.
✉ The Esplanade, Petone, Lower Hutt ☎ 04 568 4199 🕐 Daily 10:30AM–10PM

Fujiyama Teppanyaki (£££)
Good Japanese hot-plate-style restaurant.
✉ 36 Taranaki Street ☎ 04 801 8699 🕐 Lunch & dinner daily

Grain of Salt (£££)
Fine dining with harbour views; mainly New Zealand cuisine.
✉ 232 Oriental Parade ☎ 04 384 8642 🕐 Lunch Mon–Fri, dinner daily

Il Casino (££)
Top Italian-style food in downtown area.
✉ 108 Tory Street ☎ 04 385 7496 🕐 Lunch & dinner daily

Kimble Bent's (£££)
Top hotel dining at the Parkroyal Hotel.
✉ Corner Featherston & Grey streets ☎ 04 472 2722 🕐 Lunch Mon–Fri, dinner Mon–Sat

Kircaldie & Stains (£)
'The Birdcage' restaurant in Wellington's leading department store.
✉ 165–177 Lambton Quay ☎ 04 472 5899 🕐 Mon–Fri 9:30–4:30, Sat 10–3

The Lido (££)
Busy café, opposite the information centre, for breakfast and lunch.
✉ Corner Victoria & Wakefield streets ☎ 04 499 6666 🕐 Mon–Sat

National Library Café (££)
Light meals at New Zealand's leading library.
✉ 58–78 Molesworth Street, Central Wellington ☎ 04 474 3000 🕐 Mon–Fri 9:30–4

Petit Lyon (£££)
Award-winning restaurant with fine cuisine.
✉ 33 Vivian Street ☎ 04 384 9402 🕐 Dinner Mon–Sat

Zino's Restaurant (££)
Award-winning seafood cuisine.
✉ 351 The Parade, Island Bay ☎ 04 383 8256 🕐 Lunch Sun–Fri, dinner daily

Napier

Bayswater (££)
Small award-winning restaurant with a view over the beach.
✉ Hardinge Road, Ahuriri
☎ 06 835 8517 🕔 Lunch & dinner daily

Beaches (££)
Popular restaurant in the old war memorial building.
✉ Marine Parade ☎ 06 835 8180 🕔 Lunch Wed–Fri, dinner Mon–Sat

East Pier (££)
Popular new brasserie at Port Ahuriri.
✉ Hardinge Road, Ahuriri
☎ 06 834 0035 🕔 Lunch & dinner daily

Harbour View (££)
Bar and brasserie at Harbour View Motor Lodge, 2km from city centre.
✉ 80b Hardinge Road, Ahuriri
☎ 06 835 8077 🕔 Breakfast, lunch & dinner daily

Marie la Rose (££)
New Zealand produce with an international flavour.
✉ 367 Gloucester Street, Taradale ☎ 06 844 5343
🕔 Dinner Mon–Sat

Peak House (££)
Restaurant and bar on the slopes of Te Mata Peak.
✉ Te Mata Peak Road, Havelock North ☎ 06 877 8663
🕔 Lunch Wed–Mon, dinner Wed–Sun

Pierre Sur le Quay (££)
French provincial-style award-winner, 2km from city centre.
✉ 62 West Quay, Ahuriri
☎ 06 834 0189 🕔 Dinner Tue–Sat, brunch & lunch Wed–Sun

New Plymouth

André L'Escargot (££)
Award-winning French provincial restaurant.
✉ 37 Brougham Street
☎ 06 758 4812 🕔 11AM–late Mon–Sat

Citadel Café (££)
International and ethnic cuisine in a peaceful atmosphere.
✉ 40 Powerham Street ☎ 06 758 8661 🕔 Lunch & dinner daily

Devon Hotel (££)
A seafood smorgasbord with meat, vegetarian and oriental dishes.
✉ 390 Devon Street East
☎ 06 759 9099 🕔 Dinner daily, music at weekends

Gables (££)
Country cooking on the edge of town, with a coffee shop and smorgasbord.
✉ Corner Waihi Road & Fantham Street ☎ 06 278 8153
🕔 9:30–4 Mon–Fri, dinner Wed–Sun

Gareth's (££)
Elegant restaurant with a long-standing reputation for freshly prepared, imaginative dishes, fine wines and good service.
✉ 182 Devon Street ☎ 06 758 5104 🕔 Lunch Mon–Fri, dinner daily

Juliana's (££)
Fine dining and service at the Auto Lodge Motor Inn.
✉ 393 Devon Street ☎ 06 758 8044 🕔 Dinner Mon–Sat

Ratanui (££)
Fully licensed restaurant in tranquil grounds.
✉ 498 Carrington Road ☎ 06 753 4002 🕔 Dinner daily

A *Hangi*
A Maori *hangi* is a method of cooking on heated stones in an earth oven. Traditionally, the food is sandwiched between leaves, sprinkled with water and then steamed. Some resort hotels and tour operators offer this option, usually in conjunction with a Maori song and dance performance. At some places the food may be precooked before being finished off *hangi*-style.

Upper South Island

Wineries
Grapes are grown in west Auckland, the Waikato district north of Hamilton, around Gisborne and Napier, at Martinborough near Wellington, in Nelson, in Canterbury, and central Otago. The premier wine-producing district, however, is regarded as the region around Blenheim in Marlborough. Wine Trail brochures are provided by the local tourist offices in these regions, giving the locations and opening hours of the vineyards.

Christchurch

Annie's Wine Bar and Restaurant (££)
Classic surroundings; jazz on Sunday evenings.
✉ Arts Centre, 2 Worcester Boulevard ☎ 03 365 0566
🕐 Lunch Mon–Sat 11:30–3, dinner daily 6–10PM

Camelot (£££)
A medieval castle-style dining room offering fine food and service.
✉ 189 Deans Avenue ☎ 03 348 8999 🕐 Dinner daily

Canterbury Tales (£££)
Award-winning restaurant of Parkroyal Hotel, with a medieval theme, offering dishes prepared from the freshest Canterbury produce, and an extensive wine list.
✉ Corner Kilmore & Durham streets ☎ 03 365 7799
🕐 Lunch Mon–Fri, dinner Mon–Sat

Christchurch Gondola Restaurant (£££)
Dining with fantastic views at a price atop the gondola cable-way.
✉ Mount Cavendish Gondola, 10 Bridle Path Road, Heathcote ☎ 03 384 4914 🕐 Lunch & dinner daily

Dux del Lux (£–££)
Very popular establishment with self-service vegetarian restaurant, Tapas Seafood Bar and Tavern Bar serving beers brewed on site.
✉ Hereford & Montreal Streets ☎ 03 366 6919
🕐 Lunch & dinner daily

Espresso 124 (££)
Light meals throughout the day and evening.
✉ 124 Oxford Terrace ☎ 03 365 0547 🕐 Daily. Closed Sun

Il Felice (££)
Italian food and décor in downtown Christchurch.
✉ 56 Lichfield Street ☎ 03 366 7535 🕐 Dinner Mon–Sat

French Farm Winery (££)
Award-winning restaurant in winery on Banks Peninsula.
✉ French Farm, Duvauchelle, Akaroa Harbour ☎ 03 304 5784
🕐 Daily 10AM–5PM

Palazzo del Marinaio (££)
Seafood and other dishes in the city centre.
✉ The Shades, 108 Hereford Street ☎ 03 365 4640
🕐 Lunch Mon–Fri, dinner daily

Sign of the Takahe (£££)
Elegant dining 6km out of Christchurch in a mock baronial castle. Seafood a specialitiy.
✉ Dyers Pass Road, Cashmere Hills ☎ 03 332 4052 🕐 Lunch daily, dinner Mon–Sat

Strawberry Fare (££)
Mouthwatering desserts are the speciality of this downtown restaurant. As well as desserts, savoury meals are served throughout the day.
✉ 114 Peterborough Street ☎ 03 365 4897 🕐 Daily

Thomas Edmonds (££)
Neat dining in a converted band rotunda next to the Avon River. New Zealand specialities complemented by home-made desserts.
✉ 230 Cambridge Terrace ☎ 03 365 2888 🕐 Lunch Sun–Fri, dinner Mon–Sat

Waitangi Restaurant (£££)
Up-market dining at Noahs Hotel, in the city centre.
✉ Oxford Terrace ☎ 03 379 4700 🕐 Dinner Mon–Sat

Blenheim

Henry Dodson's (££)
Restaurant in garden setting.
✉ 1 Dodson Street ☎ 03 577
6634 ⏰ Lunch & dinner
Mon–Sat

Hunter's Vintner's (££)
Marlborough's food and wine
served in an award-winning
vineyard, 8km from
Blenheim.
✉ Hunter's Vineyard, Rapaura
Road ☎ 03 572 8803
⏰ Lunch & dinner daily

Seymours (££)
Nice offerings of some of
Marlborough's gourmet foods
at the Blenheim Country
Lodge. Wine list has over 70
wines produced in the area.
✉ Corner Henry & Alfred
streets ☎ 03 578 5079
⏰ Lunch & dinner daily

D'Urville (££)
Local reputation for good
food.
✉ 52 Queen Street, Blenheim
☎ 03 577 9944 ⏰ Lunch
Mon–Fri, dinner daily

Kaikoura

Caves Restaurant (££)
Good value restaurant
serving snacks and local
seafoods.
✉ Main Highway South
☎ 03 319 5023 ⏰ Daily from
7AM

Mount Cook

Panorama Room (£££)
Main dining room of The
Hermitage Hotel, with alpine
views.
✉ Mount Cook Village ☎ 03
435 1809 ⏰ Dinner daily

Nelson

Appelman's Restaurant (££)
A Lamb Award winner also
serving Nelson seafood,
pasta, omelettes and salads.
✉ 38 Bridge Street ☎ 03 546
8105 ⏰ Dinner daily

Broccoli Row (££)
Quality seafood and
vegetarian restaurant.
✉ 5 Baxton Square, Nelson
☎ 03 548 9621 ⏰ Lunch &
dinner Mon–Sat

Quayside (££)
Family restaurant for Nelson
seafood and general cuisine.
✉ Wakefield Quay ☎ 03 548
3319 ⏰ Continuous from
11:30AM, Sun from 9AM

Ribbetts (££)
More Nelson seafood and
produce, 3km out in
Tahunanui suburb.
✉ 20 Tahunahui Drive ☎ 03
548 6911 ⏰ Dinner daily

Picton

Marlborough Terranean (££)
Fine local foods with a
European touch.
✉ 31 High Street, Picton
☎ 03 573 7122 ⏰ Dinner
Tue–Sat

Portage Hotel (££)
Take a cruise from Picton to
this beachfront restaurant for
lunch with a view.
✉ Linkwater–Kenepuru Road,
or 10:15AM Beachcomber cruise
from Picton ☎ 03 57 34309
⏰ Hotel serves three meals
daily; cruise lunch only

Westland

Blue Ice Café(££)
Good, varied international
fare amid glacier country.
Delicious desserts and good
espresso coffee. Jazz music.
✉ SH6, Franz Josef Glacier
Village ☎ 03 752 0707
⏰ Three meals daily. Closed in
winter

Wild Foods Festival
Held at Hokitika in early
March, this festival is an
annual extravaganza of
gourmet bush-tucker,
based on the West
Coast's natural food
sources. The emphasis is
on novel, tasty and healthy
dishes using natural, wild
food. As well as the food
and drink, continuous
entertainment takes place
all afternoon.

Lower South Island

Wine and Food Festivals

The annual Marlborough Wine and Food Festival, centred on Blenheim in the second or third weekend of February, is the leading event of this kind in the country. Similar festivals celebrating the pleasures of eating and drinking are held at Wellington, Christchurch, Martinborough near Wellington, and Auckland's suburb of Devonport.

Queenstown

Avanti (££)
Italian and local foods in the centre of town. Relaxed atmosphere and good service.
🖂 **20 The Mall** ☎ **03 442 8503**
🕘 **Lunch & dinner daily**

Bentley's Brasserie (£££)
First-rate food and views at the Queenstown Parkroyal Hotel.
🖂 **Beach Street** ☎ **03 442 7800** 🕘 **10–10 daily**

Berkel's (£–££)
Renowned for its burgers – huge choice of fillings. Extensive list of beers and wines.
🖂 **19 Shotover Street** ☎ **03 442 6950** 🕘 **Daily**

The Cow (£)
Unlikely name for very popular pizza café. Roaring fire on chilly evenings. Book in advance or expect to have a long wait.
🖂 **Cow Lane** ☎ **03 442 8588**
🕘 **Dinner daily**

Eichardts Tavern (£)
Pub meals in the mall.
🖂 **The Mall** ☎ **03 442 8369**
🕘 **Lunch & dinner daily**

Gantley's (££)
Reputation for good food and service in an out of town renovated ruin.
🖂 **Arthurs Point Road** ☎ **03 442 8999** 🕘 **Lunch & dinner daily**

Gibbston Valley Vineyard (££)
Pleasant dining 11km out of town at one of the world's southernmost vineyards.
🖂 **Main Highway 6, Queenstown** ☎ **03 442 6910** 🕘 **Lunch daily**

Minami Jujisei (££)
Supposedly the world's southernmost Japanese restaurant, with a large variety of Japanese dishes. Sushi bar, traditional Tatami room and Western-style dining room.
🖂 **45 Beach Street** ☎ **03 442 9854** 🕘 **Lunch Mon–Fri, dinner daily**

Nugget Point Retreat (£££)
New Zealand fine food served well at this hotel overlooking the Shotover River gorge, 6km out of Queenstown.
🖂 **Arthurs Point Road** ☎ **03 442 7273** 🕘 **Dinner daily**

Promenade (££)
Nice dining near town centre. Excellent service and dishes, many featuring New Zealand lamb.
🖂 **Gardens Parkroyal, Marine Parade** ☎ **03 442 7750**
🕘 **Three meals daily**

Reflections (££)
Excellent value fixed-price Sunday buffet.
🖂 **Holiday Inn Resort, Salisbury Road, Fernhill** ☎ **03 442 6600** 🕘 **Lunch and dinner daily; Sunday buffet 11:30–2**

Skyline Restaurant (££)
Ride the cable gondola for great views and good food, then relax in the lounge with a sundowner cocktail.
🖂 **Take gondola in Brecon Street** ☎ **03 442 7860**
🕘 **Dinner daily**

The Stables (££)
Fine dining in converted stables at historic Arrowtown, 20km from Queenstown.
🖂 **22 Buckingham Street, Arrowtown** ☎ **03 442 1818**
🕘 **Dinner daily in summer, Wed–Sun in winter**

Dunedin

Bell Pepper Blues (££)
Award-winner with good food American style.
✉ 474 Princes Street ☎ 03 474 0973 🕐 Lunch Wed–Fri, dinner Mon–Sat

Cargill's Restaurant (£££)
French cuisine in a pleasant setting at Cargills Motor Inn.
✉ 678 George Street ☎ 03 477 7983 🕐 Lunch & dinner daily

Ninety Five (££)
Modern menu with local foods.
✉ 95 Filleul Street ☎ 03 471 9265 🕐 Dinner daily, brunch on Sunday

Portraits Restaurant (££)
Award-winning fare at Abbey Lodge, 2km from city centre.
✉ 900 Cumberland.Street ☎ 03 477 5380 🕐 Lunch Mon–Fri, dinner daily

Ports of Call (££)
Hotel dining room in downtown.
✉ Southern Cross Hotel, 118 High Street ☎ 03 477 0752 🕐 Dinner daily

Terrace Café(££)
New Zealand, Mediterranean and vegetarian dishes.
✉ 118 Moray Place ☎ 03 47 40686 🕐 Dinner Tue–Sat

Invercargill

Birchwoods Brasserie (££)
Carvery and à la carte dining at Ascot Park Hotel.
✉ Corner Tay Street & Racecourse Road ☎ 03 217 6195 🕐 Usual hotel meal hours with extended evening times

Donovan (££)
Fine foods in an old homestead.

✉ 220 Bainfield Road ☎ 03 215 8156 🕐 Dinner Tue–Sun

Stirling Point Tea-rooms and Restaurant (££)
Choice of snacks or meals at this southernmost point.
✉ Stirling Point, Bluff ☎ 03 212 8855

Te Anau

Baileys (££)
Café serving sandwiches to seafood.
✉ Main Street ☎ 03 249 7526 🕐 Lunch through dinner; reduced hours in winter

McKinnon Room (££)
Elegant dining at the Te Anau Travelodge Hotel.
✉ Lake Front Drive ☎ 03 249 7411 🕐 Dinner daily

La Toscana (££)
Tuscan cooking in central Te Anau.
✉ 108 Town Centre ☎ 03 249 7756 🕐 Dinner Mon–Sat

Wanaka

Amigos (££)
Casual coffee or dinner from Mexico.
✉ 34a Ardmore Street ☎ 03 443 7872 🕐 Tue–Sun from 6PM

Cardrona Tavern (£)
Bistro by day, restaurant at night, in historic goldfields pub built in 1860s.
✉ Crown Range Road, Cardrona Valley (29km from Wanaka) ☎ 03 443 8153 🕐 Lunch daily, dinner Wed–Sun

Relishes Café (£)
International and New Zealand fare.
✉ 99 Ardmore Street ☎ 03 443 9018 🕐 Daily 9AM–3PM, then 6:30–late. Closed Tue in winter

Cobb & Co
This was the name of the first South Island horse and coach company, providing transport around the island on a number of set routes before the days of the railway and motorcar. Their name is remembered in a chain of restaurants.

Tipping and Tax
As a rule, tipping for any sort of service is not a common practice in New Zealand and is not expected. However, if the service has been exceptional, a tip will not be refused.

Always check the menu to see whether GST tax (▶ 104) is included in or is additional to the prices quoted.

Upper North Island

Prices
Prices are for a double
room, excluding breakfast
and GST (► 104).

£ = single or double
rooms at less than
$50
££ = $50–150
£££ = over $150,
including GST

Auckland
**Auckland Airport
Travelodge (£££)**
International standard, 4km
from airport.
✉ Corner Kirkbride & Ascot
Road, Mangere ☎ 09 275 1059
🚌 Transfer from airport on
request

**Auckland Central
Backpackers (£)**
Hostel in city centre.
✉ 9 Fort Street ☎ 09 358
4877

Barrycourt Motor Inn (££)
Many rooms with kitchens.
✉ 10–20 Gladstone Road,
Parnell ☎ 09 303 3789

Novotel Auckland (£££)
Central city location; 188
rooms.
✉ Customs Street ☎ 09 377
8920

**Remuera Motor Lodge &
Inner City Motor Camp (£)**
Budget accommodation and
motor camp, 9km from city.
✉ 16 Minto Road, Remuera
☎ 09 5245126

**Sedgewick Kent Lodge
(£££)**
Luxury suburban bed and
breakfast homestead.
✉ 65 Lucerne Road, Remuera
☎ 09 524 5219

Sky City Hotel (£££)
New hotel, conference
centre and casino, adjacent
to the Sky Tower in central
Auckland.
✉ Corner Victoria & Federal
Streets ☎ 09 912 6000

**Stamford Plaza Auckland
(£££)**
Considered Auckland's top
hotel, in heart of central
business district.

✉ Albert Street ☎ 09 309
8888

Bay of Islands
Autolodge Hotel (££)
Central location; 72 rooms.
✉ 8 Marsden Road, Paihia
☎ 09 402 7416

**Quality Resort Waitangi
(£££)**
Coastal location with
recreational areas.
✉ Tau Henare Drive, Waitangi
☎ 09 402 7411

Rotorua
Aywon Motel (££)
Motel with full kitchens,
opposite Sheraton.
✉ 18–20 Trigg Avenue ☎ 07
347 7659

**Regal Geyserland Hotel
(££)**
Views of Whakarewarewa
thermal area.
✉ Fenton Street ☎ 07 348
2039

**Royal Lakeside Novotel
(£££)**
New international hotel
adjacent to lake.
✉ 9–11 Tutanekai Street
☎ 07 346 3888

Taupo
Oasis Beach Resort (££)
Lakeside motor inn, 3km
from central Taupo.
✉ 241 Lake Terrace ☎ 07
378 9339

Tui Oaks Motor Inn (££)
Four-storey motel by the lake.
✉ 88 Lake Terrace ☎ 07 378
8305

Wairakei Resort (£££)
Upgraded property in Thermal
Valley. Golf, tennis, spa.
✉ State Highway 1, Wairakei
☎ 07 374 8485

Lower North Island

Wellington

Airport Hotel (££)
Located just four minutes from Wellington airport, 120 rooms.

✉ **16 Kemp Street** ☎ **04 387 2189**

Burma Motor Lodge (££)
Suburban hotel 10 minutes by car from city; 63 rooms.

✉ **Burma Road, Johnsonville** ☎ **04 478 4909** 🏠 **Raroa**

Hotel Raffaele (£££)
Waterfront boutique hotel.

✉ **36 Oriental Parade, Oriental Bay** ☎ **04 384 3450**

James Cook Central (£££)
Downtown business and tourist hotel.

✉ **147 The Terrace** ☎ **04 499 9500**

Plaza International (£££)
International standard, handily placed with views over the harbour.

✉ **148 Wakefield Street** ☎ **04 473 3900**

Portland Towers (££)
Centrally located with 107 units.

✉ **24 Hawkestone Street, Thorndon** ☎ **04 473 2208**

Trekkers Hotel/Motel (££)
Budget accommodation with facility and non-facility rooms and motel units.

✉ **213 Cuba Street** ☎ **04 385 2153**

Wellington Parkroyal Hotel (£££)
Central international hotel.

✉ **Grey Street** ☎ **04 472 2722**

West Plaza Hotel (£££)
Centrally located; 102 rooms.

✉ **110–116 Wakefield Street** ☎ **04 473 1440**

Napier

Edgewater Motor Lodge (££)
Motel-style, adjacent to city centre and promenade. Rooms vary from studio units to executive suites, saltwater plunge pool, laundry and games room.

✉ **359 Marine Parade** ☎ **06 835 1148**

Kennedy Park Holiday Complex (£)
Motels, tourist flats, cabins and campsites in suburban park-like grounds.

✉ **Storkey Street** ☎ **06 843 9126**

The Master's Lodge (££)
Very small up-market lodge on Bluff Hill with superb views.

✉ **10 Elizabeth Road, Bluff Hill** ☎ **06 834 1946**

Tennyson Motor Inn (££)
Central city location; 42 units.

✉ **Corner Clive Square & Tennyson Street** ☎ **06 835 3373**

New Plymouth

Amber Court Motel (££)
Five minutes' walk to city centre and close to Pukekura Park, 32 units with kitchens, heated pool.

✉ **61 Eliot Street** ☎ **06 758 0922**

Devon Hotel (££)
Centrally located with 100 rooms.

✉ **390 Devon Street East** ☎ **06 759 9099**

Flamingo Motel (££)
A New Zealand Automobile Association award-winner with 30 self-contained units.

✉ **355 Devon Street** ☎ **06 758 8149**

Motels

Motels in New Zealand are generally a most acceptable form of accommodation. They usually have kitchen (self-catering) facilities in each room unit rather than a central dining room, although breakfast may be provided to units on request.

Upper South Island

Holiday Parks
The term holiday park usually indicates a camping ground for both tents and motorhomes and there are usually a number of cabins and/or tourist flats for rent as well. Guests may be required to provide their own bed-linen, cutlery and utensils. Facilities such as washing rooms and lighting range from the basic to the quite luxurious.

Christchurch
Airport Plaza Christchurch Hotel (£££)
Near the airport; 156 rooms
✉ **Memorial Avenue** ☎ **03 358 3139** ✈ **Airport**

Latimer Lodge (££)
Ninety units, including 40 new luxury suites, in walking distance of downtown.
✉ **30 Latimer Square**
☎ **03 379 6760**

Noahs Christchurch (£££)
Smart city centre hotel.
✉ **Corner Worcester Street & Oxford Terrace** ☎ **03 379 4700**

Quality Hotel Durham Street(££)
One of three Quality chain properties in Christchurch.
✉ **Corner Durham & Kilmore streets** ☎ **03 365 4699**

Raceway Motel (££)
Units with kitchens, handy to station.
✉ **222 Lincoln Road, Addington** ☎ **03 338 0511**

Spencer Park Holiday Park (£)
About 300 camp sites, also flats, cabins and a lodge.
✉ **Heyders Road, Spencerville** ☎ **03 329 8721**

Stonehurst Backpackers (£)
Dormitory and two-person accommodation, five minutes' walk from city centre. Breakfast available.
✉ **241 Gloucester Street** ☎ **03 379 4620**

Blenheim
Blenheim Country Lodge (££)
Three minutes' walk from town centre.
✉ **Corner Alfred & Henry streets** ☎ **03 578 5079.**

Mount Cook
The Hermitage Hotel (£££)
Well-established hotel of standing in Mount Cook National Park.
✉ **Mount Cook Village, South Canterbury** ☎ **03 435 1809**

Mount Cook Motels & Chalets (££)
Eighteen units with cooking facilities. Operated in conjunction with The Hermitage.
✉ **Mount Cook Village, South Canterbury** ☎ **03 435 1809**

Nelson
AA Motor Lodge (££)
Non-smoking units with kitchen facilities; near city centre.
✉ **8 Ajax Avenue** ☎ **03 548 8214**

Quality Hotel Rutherford (££)
High standard of accommodation, adjacent to central city. Restaurant & bar.
✉ **Trafalgar Square** ☎ **03 548 2299**

Westland National Park
Fox Glacier Holiday Park (£)
Cabins, flats and lodge rooms; 800m from township.
✉ **Lake Mathieson Road, Fox Glacier** ☎ **03 751 0821**

Franz Josef Glacier Hotel (£££)
Refurbished rooms (147) in Franz Josef township.
✉ **State Highway 6, Franz Josef** ☎ **03 752 0729**

Terrace Motel (££)
Ten units with kitchen facilities, five minutes' walk to village.
✉ **Cowan Street, Franz Josef Glacier**
☎ **03 752 0130**

Lower South Island

Queenstown

Gardens Parkroyal Hotel (£££)
On Lake Wakatipu waterfront, adjacent to shopping area.
✉ **Corner Earl Street & Marine Parade** ☎ 03 442 7750

Lakeland Hotel (£££)
Well-appointed rooms overlooking lake.
✉ **14–18 Lake Esplanade** ☎ 03 442 7600

Queenstown Motor Park (£)
Campsites, cabins, flats, lodge, with views.
✉ **51 Man Street** ☎ 03 442 7252

Queenstown Parkroyal Hotel (£££)
Overlooking the lake and near the town centre.
✉ **Beach Street** ☎ 03 442 7800

Remarkables Resort Hotel (££)
Sixty units with views, 6km from Queenstown.
✉ **14 Yewlett Crescent, Frankton** ☎ 03 442 2080

St James Apartments (££)
Quality accommodation in one- and two-bedroom units.
✉ **Coronation Drive** ☎ 03 442 5333

Spinnaker Bay Apartments (£££)
Luxury one-, two- and three-bedroom units, with kitchens.
✉ **101 Frankton Road** ☎ 03 442 7827

Dunedin

Abbey Lodge (££)
Twelve self-contained units and 38 hotel rooms; 2km from city centre.
✉ **900 Cumberland Street** ☎ 03 477 5380

Garden Motel (££)
Twelve-unit motel with cooking facilities; 2km from city centre.
✉ **958 George Street** ☎ 03 477 8251

Leviathan Hotel (££)
Near the station; 77 rooms.
✉ **27 Queens Gardens** ☎ 03 477 3160

Southern Cross Hotel (£££)
City centre location; 134 rooms.
✉ **Corner Princes & High streets** ☎ 03 477 0752

Invercargill

Ascot Park Hotel (££)
Seventy hotel rooms and 24 motel units five minutes' walk from city centre.
✉ **Corner Tay Street & Racecourse Road** ☎ 03 217 6195

Surrey Court Motels (££)
Ten-unit motel with cooking facilities.
✉ **400 Tay Street** ☎ 03 217 6102

Te Anau

Luxmore Hotel Lodge (££)
Town centre hotel.
✉ **Main Street** ☎ 03 249 7526

Te Anau Travelodge (£££)
International hotel near lake.
✉ **Lake Front Drive** ☎ 03 249 7411

Wanaka

Edgewater Resort (£££)
Rooms (100) with balconies.
✉ **Sargood Drive** ☎ 03 443 8311

Te Wanaka Lodge (££)
Luxurious B&B.
✉ **23 Brownston Street** ☎ 03 443 9224

Booking Ahead
Regardless of your choice of accommodation, remember that the summer season, from October through to April, is the busiest time. Most hotels are full in February and March, and most motels tend to be full in December and January. Booking ahead for these months at least, as well as during New Zealand's school and public holidays (➤ 116), is advised.

Major Shopping Districts

With or Without Tax?
New Zealand has a Goods and Services Tax (GST) of 12.5 per cent, applicable to all goods purchased, including food and accommodation. In general, this tax is included in the price stated unless (by law) otherwise indicated. However, it is always as well to check that the price is inclusive, particularly at some of the more expensive hotels and restaurants. Some of the guided walking tours may also advertise prices without tax.

Auckland and Upper North Island
Auckland's main downtown shopping thoroughfare is Queen Street, running from Queen Elizabeth II Square at the Ferry Building to Aotea Square with its Aotea Centre and Town Hall. The major hotels, airline offices, banks, shops, postal facilities, central library, art gallery, cinemas, concert halls and visitor information centres are in or adjacent to this street.

There are also many suburban shopping precincts in the city, with Newmarket and the St Lukes Mall in the suburb of Mount Albert being of interest.

In the upper North Island, Rotorua and Taupo have quite large and interesting downtown shopping areas and are premier tourist areas with many souvenir and duty-free shops.

Wellington and Lower North Island
The capital's main shopping street is Lambton Quay, but Willis Street, Manners Street and Cuba Street are also of interest, with partial mall development. There is an underground shopping centre at the corner of Lambton Quay and Willis Street. Post offices, banks, libraries, theatres and visitor information centres are close by.

Napier offers a smart downtown shopping area, including some traffic-free streets.

In New Plymouth shopping is centred on its main street (Devon Street), part of which is traffic-restricted. One block north, the City Centre Mall offers enclosed shopping.

Christchurch and Upper South Island
Cathedral Square marks the centre of downtown Christchurch, with Colombo Street and Cashel Street (City Mall) being the main shopping thoroughfares. Other side streets are also of interest, however. Commercial facilities, including post offices and banks, are also in this area.

To the north of the square, in Colombo Street, there are many tourist and souvenir shops and a visitor information office is situated beside the Avon River in Worcester Street.

Christchurch's largest suburban shopping area is at Riccarton, where there is both street-side and mall shopping.

In the upper South Island both Blenheim and Nelson have vibrant downtown shopping areas.

Queenstown and Lower South Island
Queenstown, in the lower South Island, is a major tourist centre and many of the shops in its compact downtown area are visitor orientated. It is also the only place in New Zealand where major stores and boutiques stay open until 10PM daily.

Dunedin, a city with a much larger resident population, has many good shops in George and Princes streets, on either side of the Octagon reserve.

Invercargill has a modest downtown shopping area. Te Anau and Wanaka, both small towns, have fairly limited shopping. However, both offer interesting browsing for travellers.

Departmental & Clothing Stores

Auckland

Action Downunder
High-quality outdoor clothing.
✉ 75 Queen Street (and branches) ☎ 09 309 0241

Canterbury of New Zealand
New Zealand clothing, specialising in All Black rugby team labels.
✉ Corner Queen & Customs streets (and other branches)
☎ 09 379 4937

Kathmandu
Popular New Zealand clothing label, specialising in outdoor wear.
✉ 350 Queen Street ☎ 09 309 4615

Saks
A fashionable shop for men's clothing, 4km from centre.
✉ 254 Broadway, Newmarket
☎ 09 520 7630

Smith & Caughey Ltd
Fine department store, including clothing.
✉ 253–261 Queen Street
☎ 09 377 4770

Victoria Park Market
New Zealand's largest selection of T-shirts.
✉ Victoria Street West

Wellington

Bresolini
High Italian and New Zealand fashion.
✉ 108 Tory Street ☎ 04 801 9459

Destiny Extreme Sports
Sports equipment and gear.
✉ 55 Cuba Street ☎ 04 499 8962

Kircaldie & Stains Ltd
Elegant department store.
✉ 165–177 Lambton Quay
☎ 04 472 5899

Skin Things
Leather clothes and accessories.
✉ Corner Cuba & Manners streets ☎ 04 802 4169

Christchurch

Ballantynes
Popular department store with large variety of merchandise.
✉ City Mall, 130 Cashel Street
☎ 03 379 7400

Bresolini
Many fashionable labels.
✉ 90 Hereford Street ☎ 03 379 0674

Milano Men
Menswear fashion clothing, both imported and from New Zealand.
✉ Guthrey Centre, 126 Cashel Street Mall ☎ 03 365 5409

Rowlands of Christchurch
High-quality New Zealand and overseas clothes.
✉ Merivale Mall, 185 Papanui Road, Merivale ☎ 03 355 5045

Queenstown

Canterbury of New Zealand
New Zealand clothing, specialising in All Black rugby team labels.
✉ O'Connells Shopping Centre
☎ 03 442 4020

T and Ski
Kiwi-style leisurewear.
✉ Two locations, including the Mall ☎ 03 442 9817

Dunedin

Arthur Barnett Ltd
Older, established department store with an array of ladies' and men's clothing, household furnishings and giftware.
✉ 207 George Street ☎ 03 477 1129

Chain Stores
In New Zealand, the Woolworths name is applied to a chain of grocery supermarkets. The goods and services associated with the name in other countries can be found at Deka stores. The Warehouse chain operates as a discount operation, with a wide variety of general merchandise. Most cities and towns also have a Farmers shop, offering a large range of household goods and clothing. K-Mart stores, selling similar stock, are found in many major suburbs and towns.

New Zealand Labels
Internationally recognised New Zealand labels are always in demand. Canterbury brand clothing is popular, as is any clothing with the insignia of the All Blacks rugby team. Swanndri and Kathmandu are two recognised outdoor clothing labels. Zeal, Country Road, Hot Buttered and Origin are other 'down-under' labels sought by the young at heart.

Books, Magazines & Music

Bookshops
Whitcoulls have branches in all cities and major suburbs, as do London Books. Paper Plus is a franchise chain. The larger cities usually have a number of specialist bookstores carrying selected subjects. Second-hand bookshops in towns tend to stock mainly paperbacks, whereas in the larger cities second-hand hardbacks can also be found.

Music Shops
All towns have one or more shops selling CDs and cassettes. As well as the usual range, Maori and Polynesian music is available in both formats. Sounds is a chain of music shops in many North Island locations. Records are not widely sold, but second-hand records, along with used tapes and CDs, can be found in the country's three main cities.

Auckland
Dorothy Butler Bookshop
Children's books and crafts.
✉ **Corner Jervois & St Marys Bay Road, Ponsonby** ☎ **09 3767 283**

Dymocks
Main Auckland store for large Australian bookseller.
✉ **Atrium on Elliott, 21 Elliott Street** ☎ **09 379 9919**

Parsons
Specialist books on the arts and New Zealand.
✉ **New Gallery Building, Wellesley Sreet** ☎ **09 303 1557**

Pathfinder
Specialist bookstore for psychology and wellbeing.
✉ **New Gallery Building, Wellesley Street** ☎ **09 379 0147**

Rare Books
One of Auckland's better stores for used non-fiction.
✉ **6 High Street** ☎ **09 379 0379**

Wellington
Arty Bee's
Popular second-hand bookstore on all subjects.
✉ **158 Cuba Street** ☎ **04 384 5339**

Bennetts
Book shop for government and New Zealand publications, affiliated with Whitcoulls chain.
✉ **Bowen House, corner Lambton Quay & Bowen Street** ☎ **04 499 3433**

Unity Books
Specialist retailer for arts and intellectual titles.
✉ **Westpac Life House, 119–125 Willis Street** ☎ **04 38 56110**

Christchurch
Scorpio Books
Mainly, but not exclusively, arts and serious topics.
✉ **Corner Hereford Street & Oxford Terrace** ☎ **03 379 2882**

UBS University Book Shop
For both students and public; a wide selection of topics.
✉ **University Drive, Ilam** ☎ **03 384 8679**

CDs and Tapes

Auckland
Marbecks
Auckland's top store for serious listening.
✉ **Three locations: two in Queens Arcade, 36 Queen Street** ☎ **09 379 0444**

Real Groovy Records
Selection of new and used records, cassettes and CDs.
✉ **438 Queen Street** ☎ **09 377 5870**

Wellington
Allan's Compact Discs Ltd
General catalogue of most popular and classical works.
✉ **AA Centre, 342–352 Lambton Quay** ☎ **04 499 7675**

Parsons Books & Music
A serious bookshop with classical CDs as well.
✉ **126 Lambton Quay** ☎ **04 472 4587**

Christchurch
Echo Records
New and used CDs and cassettes.
✉ **237 High Street** ☎ **03 366 7410**

Dunedin
Disk Den
CDs and cassettes, all types.
✉ **118 Princes Street** ☎ **03 477 2280**

Handcrafts, Antiques & Markets

Auckland

Downtown Hilton Gallery
Paintings, especially those featuring New Zealand scenery.
✉ **Downtown Shopping Centre, 4 Albert Street** ☎ **09 3033836**

Elephant House
Selling a variety of craft items you didn't think you needed!
✉ **237 Parnell Road, Parnell**
☎ **09 309 8740**

International Art Centre
Art by famous artists.
✉ **272 Parnell Road, Parnell**
☎ **09 379 4101**

Otara Market
Open-air early morning market with vegetables, domestic items and general merchandise (some second-hand).
✉ **Suburb of Otara** 🕐 **Sat only**

Victoria Park Market
A permanent collection of little shops and stallholders in an old converted building several blocks from the downtown area. There is a variety of goods, especially T-shirts and other casual clothing.
✉ **Victoria Street West**

Wellington

McGregor Wright Gallery
Art dealers specialising mostly in 20th-century New Zealand artists.
✉ **Law Society Building, 26 Waring Taylor Street** ☎ **04 472 1281**

The Market
Stalls and a food hall.
✉ **James Smith building, corner Cuba & Manners streets**

Wellington Market
Over 150 stalls from Friday through Sunday.
✉ **Corner of Taranaki Street & Jervois Quay**

Walker & Hall Antiques
A jeweller and silversmith, with branches in Auckland as well.
✉ **93 The Terrace** ☎ **04 472 4259**

Christchurch

Arts Centre
A variety of shops selling arts, crafts and souvenirs all housed in a classic Gothic building. At weekends there are also a number of outside stallholders.
✉ **Worcester Boulevard**

Galleria and Arts Centre Workshop
Includes Maori carvings and hand-crafted glassware.
✉ **Arts Centre, Worcester Street** ☎ **03 366 0989**

Leisure Craft Centre
Crafts and souvenirs.
✉ **88 Worcester Street** ☎ **03 366 3940**

Queenstown

New Zealand Artisan Gallery
Artworks in precious metals, wood, glass and ceramics.
✉ **Skyline Arcade, The Mall**
☎ **03 442 9589**

Queens Gallery
Quality New Zealand fine art.
✉ **O'Connells Shopping Centre**
☎ **03 44 26063**

Dunedin

Rosslyn Gallery
Local original art and reproductions.
✉ **358 George Street** ☎ **03 477 9899**

Antiques

True antiques are rare in New Zealand and most items regarded as antique are in fact only between 40 and 80 years old. The terms second-hand and antique tend to be used rather loosely and often a good deal of the former has to be sifted through before anything of value can be found.

English dinner sets, Victorian bric-à-brac and art of all kinds are sought-after and popular collectors' items include small toys, cigarette cards, jewellery and ginger jars.

Tourist Souvenirs

Souvenirs
Generally, souvenirs of New Zealand reflect its Maori culture, its agricultural heritage and its scenery. Handcrafted items are prevalent and there are good selections of pottery, paintings, Maori-designed woodcarvings, greenstone (jade) jewellery, sheepskin rugs, woollen ware, honey, wine, placemats, books and calendars of scenic photos.

Lucky Charm
The *hei-tiki*, more often known simply as the *tiki*, is a favourite Maori souvenir. Thought possibly to have originated as a fertility symbol, its true significance has been lost in time. These days it is widely sold as a small good-luck charm, carved from either greenstone or wood.

Auckland
Aotea NZ Souvenirs
The Auckland branch of a nationwide chain.
📧 **Lower Albert Street** ☎ 09 379 5022

Auckland Museum Gift Shop
Rated as one of Auckland's best souvenir shops.
📧 **Auckland Domain, Parnell** ☎ 09 309 2580

Auckland Tourist Centre Souvenirs
Located downtown at the terminal for airport buses.
📧 **Downtown Airline Terminal, 86 Quay Street** ☎ 09 379 6289

Exclusively New Zealand
Handily located around the corner from Queen Street.
📧 **11 Customs Street East** ☎ 09 309 8642

Great New Zealand Gift Shop
Usual souvenir lines, located near foot of main street.
📧 **7 Queen Street** ☎ 09 373 5431

Wild Places
Operated by the Maruia Society this shop sells souvenirs with conservation themes.
📧 **28 Lorne Street** ☎ 09 358 0795

Wellington
Great New Zealand Shop
Covers a wide selection – sheepskin rugs, knitwear.
📧 **AMP Centre, Grey Street** ☎ 04 472 6817

Christchurch
Aotea NZ Souvenirs
The Christchurch branch of a nationwide chain.
📧 **65 Cathedral Square** ☎ 03 366 7814

Medici
Leather and sheepskin products and accessories.
📧 **95 Worcester Street** ☎ 03 366 4877

Woodcraft Gallery
Fine wood-turned and handcrafted items.
📧 **Arts Centre** ☎ 03 3656082

Queenstown
Alpine Artifacts
Local souvenirs, including clothing.
📧 **34 Queenstown Mall** ☎ 03 442 8644

Aotea Souvenirs
For all kinds of New Zealand souvenirs.
📧 **Beach Street** ☎ 03 442 6444

Dunedin
Glendermid
Lambskin rugs, woollen slippers, travel rugs, handbags.
📧 **192 Castle Street** ☎ 03 477 3655

Golden Leaf International
For various New Zealand products, jewellery and leathergoods.
📧 **16 Manse Street** ☎ 03 474 0063

New Zealand Shop
All types of souvenirs of New Zealand; can post around the world.
📧 **6 Civic Centre, Octagon** ☎ 03 477 3379

The Scottish Shop
The place in Dunedin to buy all things Scottish.
📧 **187 George Street** ☎ 03 477 9965

Tourist Information

All cities and towns have an office belonging to the Visitor Information Network, operated locally, which can provide information about and usually make bookings for attractions, tours, transport and accommodation. The offices are signposted nationally with the symbol ⓘ .

All national parks have a visitor centre run by the Department of Conservation (DoC) with information about the geography, geology, environment, flora and fauna on display, and there are details about what can be done and seen in each park, including walking routes.

The New Zealand head office of the Automobile Association is located at 99 Albert Street, Auckland. There are also a number of other offices throughout the country.

Visitor Information Offices

Upper North Island
Auckland
✉ **Aotea Square, 299 Queen Street** ☎ **09 366 6888**

Bay Of Islands
✉ **Marsden Road, Paihia**
☎ **09 402 7345**

Rotorua
✉ **67 Fenton Street**
☎ **07 348 5179**

Taupo
✉ **13 Tongariro Street**
☎ **07 378 9000**

Lower North Island
Napier
✉ **Marine Parade**
☎ **06 834 1911**

New Plymouth
✉ **Corner Liardet & Leach streets** ☎ **06 758 6080**

Wellington
✉ **101 Wakefield Street**
☎ **04 801 4000; also on Inter-island ferries operating from Wellington to Picton**

Upper South Island
Blenheim
✉ **Forum Building, Queen Street** ☎ **03 578 9904**

Christchurch
✉ **Corner Worcester Street & Oxford Terrace**
☎ **03 379 9629**

Mount Cook
✉ **Bowen Drive**
☎ **03 435 1818**

Nelson
✉ **Corner Trafalgar & Halifax streets** ☎ **03 548 2304**

Westland National Park
✉ **SH6, Franz Josef village**
☎ **03 752 0796; also at Fox Glacier** ☎ **03 751 0807**

Lower South Island
Dunedin
✉ **48 The Octagon**
☎ **03 474 3300**

Invercargill
✉ **c/o Southland Museum, Queens Park**
☎ **03 214 6243**

Queenstown
✉ **Corner Shotover & Camp streets** ☎ **03 442 4100**

Te Anau
✉ **Te Anau Terrace**
☎ **03 249 8900**

Wanaka
✉ **Ardmore Street**
☎ **03 443 1233**

Photographic Film
Major brands of photographic film can be purchased all over the country. Processing of colour prints, with a price structure related to the time taken, is also undertaken at many places. The processing of slide film is not so widespread and film will probably have to be forwarded to an appropriate laboratory.

North Island

Amusements Galore

As well as purpose-built attractions, there are numerous parks and playgrounds in New Zealand, together with plenty of cinemas, video-game parlours, bowling alleys, go-cart tracks and all sorts of other modern pastimes. However, remember that whatever children are up to in the open air, they should always be well protected from the sun.

Auckland
Fun Station

A suburban complex offering go-carts, mini-golf, ten-pin bowling and a McDonalds!
✉ **525 Ellerslie-Panmure Highway** ☎ **09 570 9130**
🕐 **Daily**

Glenbrook Vintage Railway

Steam train rides on Sundays (not winter), from Glenbrook to Waiuku.
✉ **50km south of Auckland** ☎ **09 636 9361** 🕐 **Hourly departures, 11AM–4PM**

Kelly Tarlton's Underwater World and Antarctic Experience

Live fish, sharks and penguins will entertain young and old alike.
✉ **Tamaki Drive, Orakei** ☎ **09 528 1994** 🕐 **9–6; last admission 5:30PM**

Rainbows End Adventure Park

New Zealand's best-known leisure park with rides and activities.
✉ **Wiri Station Road, Manukau** ☎ **09 262 2044**
🕐 **Daily; not evenings**

Waiwera

Hot thermal swimming pools and hydro-slides.
✉ **Waiwera Road; 48km north of Auckland on SH1** ☎ **09 426 5369** 🕐 **Daily 10AM–10PM**

Napier
Fantasyland

Children's playground.
✉ **Windsor Park, Windsor Avenue, Hastings** ☎ **06 876 0205** 🕐 **Daily**

Hawke's Bay Aquarium and Oceanarium

Displays of native and exotic species.
✉ **Marine Parade** ☎ **06 834 4196** 🕐 **9–5; feeding at 3:15PM**

Lilliput Model Railway

Display and working model town.
✉ **Marineland, Marine Parade** ☎ **06 834 4195** 🕐 **10–4:30**

Marineland of New Zealand

Sealife and shows.
✉ **Marine Parade** ☎ **06 834 4195** 🕐 **Daily 10–4:30; shows at 10:30AM and 2PM**

Rotorua
Rainbow Farm

Farm animals.
✉ **Fairy Springs Road, opposite Rainbown Springs** ☎ **07 347 8104** 🕐 **8–5; farm shows at 10:30, 11:45, 1 & 2:30**

Skyline Luge

Ride up by gondola, and then descend by luge sledge on a special pathway.
✉ **Fairy Springs Road** ☎ **07 347 0027** 🕐 **The luge is daytime only; opens 9AM**

Toot and Whistle Railway

Train rides round Kuirau Park.
✉ **Corner Ranolf & Pukuatua streets** ☎ **07 348 4133** 🕐 **Weekends & public holidays**

Taupo
Aratiatia Rapids

Water is diverted across the rocks of the old riverbed.
✉ **Aratiatia Power Station Dam, north of Wairakei** 🕐 **At 10, 12 & 2 (also 4PM in summer)**

Trainsville

Model railway display, behind a model shop on the first floor.
✉ **35a–37a Heuheu Street, downtown Taupo** ☎ **07 378 5940** 🕐 **Weekdays and Sat AM**

South Island

Christchurch
Air Force World
Aeroplanes and all sorts of other aviation items.
✉ **Air Force Museum, Main South Road, Wigram** ☎ **03 343 9532** ⏱ **10–5**

Christchurch Gondola
Ride up the Port Hills and visit the Time Tunnel at the summit.
✉ **Bridle Path Road, Heathcote** ☎ **03 384 4914** ⏱ **From 10AM**

International Antarctic Centre
Interesting display, including movies. Souvenir shop selling toy penguins etc.
✉ **Orchard Road, next to the airport** ☎ **03 358 9896** ⏱ **Daily 9:30–5:30; to 8:30PM in summer**

Orana Wildlife Park
African and native animals in natural settings.
✉ **McLeans Island Road, Harewood** ☎ **03 359 7109** ⏱ **10–4:30**

Science Alive
A hands-on display in the former railway station.
✉ **Moorhouse Avenue, about 1km from Cathedral Square** ☎ **03 372 8668**

Dunedin
Discovery World
A hands-on science centre of special interest to children.
✉ **Otago Museum, Great King Street** ☎ **03 477 2372** ⏱ **9–4:30 weekdays; Sat 10:30; Sun 1:30**

Ocean Beach Railway
Steam train rides weekends and public holidays.
✉ **St Kilda Beach** ☎ **03 455 2798** ⏱ **Times vary**

Taieri Gorge Train
A four-hour round trip through the Taieri Gorge departing most afternoons.
✉ **Dunedin Station** ☎ **03 477 4449**

Mount Cook
Glentanner Park
Farm tours, horse treks, safaris and snow excursions.
✉ **SH 80 leading in to Mount Cook** ☎ **03 435 1855**

Nelson
Nelson Ferrari Collection
Real cars and models.
✉ **Corner Collingwood Street & Selwyn Place** ☎ **03 546 6725**

Queenstown
Gondola Ride
Take the cableway up above the city.
✉ **Base station in Brecon Street** ☎ **03 442 7860** ⏱ **10–10**

Jet-Boat Rides
The most popular is the Shotover Jet, but there are other, cheaper options.
✉ **Pick-ups from downtown** ☎ **03 442 7087** ⏱ **Every 15 minutes**

Queenstown Underwater World
Step down under the water level and look out at the surrounding marine life.
✉ **Queenstown wharf (foot of The Mall)** ☎ **03 442 8437** ⏱ **9–5:30 (to 7PM in summer)**

Westland National Park
Glow-worm Grotto
A short bush walk shows glow-worm insect lights on banks and under bushes. Visit at night and take a torch.
✉ **Near the Fox Glacier village on SH6** ☎ **03 751 0807**

Child Prices
Most of the attractions listed here and elsewhere in the book offer cheaper entrance fees for children. The upper age limits vary: sometimes 12 years, sometimes 16 years.
Some transport and attractions operators also recognise International Student Identity Cards and Youth Hostel Association (YHA) membership cards.

The Auckland Card
For those who intend to pack a lot in, a card can be purchased from visitor information centres (➤ 109) in Auckland that covers entry to a number of main attractions in the city at an all-in price. It also includes harbour cruises and a bus pass. However, it is expensive.

Culture & Entertainment

Parades

Teams of marching girls in colourful get-ups are a familiar sight in New Zealand. The country's Scottish heritage is shown in the many pipe bands to be seen and there are also many brass bands.
Parades are conjured up for any event or occasion, ranging from Christmas to rugby matches.

Unique to New Zealand is the culture of the Maori, but western-style orchestral music, opera, ballet and theatre is also well represented in the main cities. Outside the towns, the largely agricultural base of New Zeland's economy is reflected in shows of a peculiarly Kiwi type, with farming made into entertainment.

A&P Shows

Distinctly agricultural and pastoral, these shows are held annually around many farming centres. Hamilton, Rotorua and Queenstown have daily tourist shows featuring farm animals, with displays ranging from milking cows to shearing sheep.

New Zealand's largest show is the National Agricultural Field Days, held for four days in the second week of June, at Mystery Creek near Hamilton.

Maori Culture

Maori concerts are given nightly in Rotorua, and also regularly in Auckland, Christchurch and Queenstown. The chants and actions of Maori warriors preparing for battle are remembered in the *haka*, while the women's *poi* dance offers a gentler form of entertainment. The *poi* is a light ball on a string which is swung to a rhythmic beat.

Performing Arts

Generally, Auckland plays host to any major European-style musical or sporting event being staged in the country and the city's status as capital ensures it is on the circuit for big-name performers from both home and abroad. There are always a number of events on.

Wellington, on the other hand, is regarded as the country's cultural capital and certainly its biennial Arts Festival, held in the autumn of even-numbered years, is a significant event featuring many famous New Zealand and international artists. Wellington is also home to the New Zealand Symphony Orchestra, and the Royal New Zealand Ballet – though both also tour other centres.

Nightlife

Generally, nightclubs cater mostly for younger adults and lack the sophistication of some overseas destinations. There are, however, casinos to be found in Auckland and Christchurch.
Many taverns and bars provide live music, including jazz.

The student population of the university cities of Auckland, Wellington, Christchurch, Dunedin, Hamilton and Palmerston North helps keep the night entertainment scene alive.

Queenstown, as the country's leading ski resort, offers a good variety of après-ski events during the winter.

Sport

Although 'rugby, racing and beer' have been considered the main sporting icons of New Zealand, all sports are popular and have large followings.

The popularity of sport with New Zealanders means that it is an essential part of the country's culture (► 114).

Cultural Activities

North Island

Auckland
Aotea Centre
Auckland's cultural centre with events ranging from orchestral concerts and theatrical shows to opera. The Auckland Town Hall, another concert venue, is adjacent.
✉ **Aotea Square, Queen Street** ☎ **What's on: 09 309 2678; tickets:** ☎ **09 307 5000**

Auckland Museum
Offers a daily display of Maori song and dance at 11AM and 1:30PM.
✉ **Auckland Domain, Cenotaph Road; 3km from downtown** ☎ **09 309 0443**

Bruce Mason Theatre
A newer venue, with a variety of local activities.
✉ **Takapuna, on Auckland's North Shore** ☎ **0800 484253 (freephone)**

Civic Theatre
Shows movies in one of the southern hemisphere's most ornate movie houses, opened in 1929.
✉ **Corner Queen & Wellesley streets** ☎ **09 377 3315**

New Plymouth
Govett-Brewster Art Gallery
Known for its contemporary paintings and kinetic sculptures.
✉ **Queen Street** ☎ **06 758 5149** ◷ **Open 10:30–5 weekdays, 1–5 weekends**

Rotorua
Rotorua's Maori Arts and Crafts Institute
Display of Maori song and dance at 12 noon each weekday, plus other Maori crafts.
✉ **Hemo Road** ☎ **07 348 9047** ◷ **Daily 8–5**

Tamaki Tours
An evening tour combining a *hangi* dinner and a Maori song and dance show in a reconstructed village setting.
✉ **Depart from Visitor Centre, Fenton Street** ☎ **07 346 2823**

Wellington
Dowse Art Museum
One of the best art galleries in the Wellington region.
✉ **Laings Road, Lower Hutt** ☎ **04 570 6500** ◷ **10–4 Mon–Fri; Sat–Sun & holidays 11–5**

Katherine Mansfield Birthplace
The house where New Zealand's best-known writer was born.
✉ **25 Tinakori Road** ☎ **04 473 7268** ◷ **Tue–Sun 10–4**

Michael Fowler Centre
The leading concert venue in Wellington.
✉ **Wakefield Street** ☎ **04 472 3088**

Wellington's Downstage Theatre
Regarded as Wellington's best playhouse.
✉ **Hannah Playhouse, Courtenay Place** ☎ **04 484 9639**

South Island

Christchurch
Christchurch Town Hall
Two concert chambers, with frequent activity, including a local orchestra.
✉ **Kilmore Street** ☎ **03 377 8899**

Court Theatre
Good productions of plays and light shows, six nights a week.
✉ **Arts Centre, 20 Worcester Street** ☎ **03 366 6992**

Television
The four national television channels are known as One, 2, TV3 and TV4. Both 2 and TV4 provide light entertainment, aimed at the younger market, while One and TV3 concentrate on current affairs and sport. All channels feature commercials.

Many of the major series from Australia, the United States and Great Britain are shown, although they will probably be running behind.

Outdoor Activities

National Favourites
Rugby is New Zealand's number one competitive sport and the national team, the All Blacks, are known internationally. Other popular winter sports include netball, soccer and hockey.

In Summer, cricket takes the limelight nationally, and lawn bowls is also a top favourite. Horse-racing and trotting (harness-racing) meetings, which attract large crowds, are held most weekends at several venues through the country.

Adventure Sports
New Zealand offers a wide variety of popular adventure and thrill activities, such as jet-boating, bungy-jumping, para-gliding and white-water rafting. While Queenstown is perhaps the home for many of these activities, several are available in other centres as well.

The South Island's Southern Alps mountain chain offers many climbing and mountaineering opportunities requiring varying degrees of skill.

Boating
This is a favourite Kiwi pastime. You can go cruising in the harbour and gulf of Auckland, the Bay of Islands, the Marlborough Sounds, the lakes of Rotorua, or the lakes and fiords of the south.

Fishing
The Rotorua and Taupo areas are famous for trout whereas parts of the South Island south of Christchurch are better known for salmon fishing.

Fishing trips, including deep-sea game fishing, are available from both Paihia and Russell.

Kaikoura, south of Blenheim, is known for its whale-watching trips.

Golf
Golf courses are prevalent. In Rotorua and Taupo thermal vents can be additional hazards. The Wairakei International Golf Course 8km north of Taupo is recognised as one of the world's best.

Horse-racing
Ellerslie Racecourse in Auckland is the city's premier racetrack. Meetings are held about every second or third Saturday; more often at holiday times. There is also trotting (harness-racing) at Alexandra Park, although Addington, in the South Island, is considered the home of trotting. The main events in Christchurch for both horse-trotting and racing are during Carnival week in November.

Skiing
The North Island's major ski-fields (July to September, sometimes longer) are on the northern and southwestern slopes of Mount Ruapehu in Tongariro National Park.

Coronet Peak and the Remarkables are Queenstown's two major ski-fields. There are more located near Wanaka. The city of Christchurch also has a number of private and club fields within two hours' drive.

Walking
The extensive and varied areas of countryside offers many walking tracks of varying lengths. Details of escorted walks or routes are available from the national park centres. It is a good idea to seek local advice before setting off alone.

Watersports
Watersports facilities of all kinds can be found through-out New Zealand, either along the extensive coast or on inland lakes and rivers. For the less energetic, swimming in the country's hot thermal springs is a pleasant option.

The Bay of Islands offers diving and snorkelling activities.

Evening Entertainment

Auckland

Civic Tavern
Offers London, Irish and Tartan bars, plus jazz several nights a week.
✉ **Corner Queen & Wellesley streets**
☎ 09 373 3684

Harrah's Sky City Casino
The largest of two casinos in New Zealand (➤ 20, Top Ten)
✉ **Corner Victoria & Federal streets**
☎ 09 912 6000

The Loaded Hog
Lively pub, serving meals, next to yacht basin.
✉ **104 Quay Street**
☎ 09 366 6491

Park in the Bar
Loud and popular with young locals and back-packers.
✉ **4 Fort Street, Central Auckland**
☎ 09 373 4742

Stanley's Bar and Nightclub
Disco for the more mature nightclubber!
✉ **192 Queen Street, Central Auckland**
☎ 09 309 0201

Wellington

Kitty O'Shea's
Live Irish music.
✉ **28 Courtenay Place** ☎ 04 385 7364

The Planet
Entertainment through to the early hours.
✉ **Corner of Courtenay Place & Tory Street** ☎ 04 382 4580

Rotorua

The Ace of Clubs
Late-night disco from Wednesday to Saturday.

✉ **Ti Street**
☎ 07 346 2204

Tamaki Tours
Offers evenings of Maori song and dance combined with a *hangi* meal (➤ 113).

Christchurch

Christchurch Casino
Poker machines and gambling tables, plus a restaurant and bars.
✉ **Victoria Street**
☎ 03 365 9999

Palladium
Disco, lights and lasers.
✉ **Chancery Lane**
☎ 03 379 0572

Queenstown

Eichardts Tavern
Jumps nightly, especially in ski season.
✉ **The Mall**
☎ 03 442 8369

McNeills Cottage Brewery
A boutique brewery and restaurant.
✉ **14 Church Street**
☎ 03 442 9688

Dunedin

Abbey Road Restaurant
Offers a nostalgic look at the great musicians of the 60s and 70s.
✉ **Moray Place**
☎ 03 477 4362

Cassidy's Saloon
For eating and drinking, near the university.
✉ **116 Albany Street**
☎ 03 477 7977

Club 118
Older bar, with disco some nights.
✉ **Southern Cross Hotel, 118 High Street**
☎ 03 477 0752

Live Music

Many New Zealand taverns and public bars feature live music in the form of a trio of electric guitars and drums. The volume is usually very loud. Jazz, less commonly, can also be found.

Altogether more sedate is the muisc played by a pianist in a handful of restaurants and some hotel lounges.

Discos, in the main cities, are numerous.

What's On When

School Holidays
Summer: mid-December to late January
May: first two weeks in May
Mid-term: middle two weeks in July
August: last week in August to second week in September

National Public Holidays
New Year (1 and 2 January)
Christmas Day (25 December)
Boxing Day (26 December)
Waitangi: National Day (6 February)
Good Friday
Easter Monday
Anzac Day: Memorial Day for War Dead (25 April)
Queen's Birthday (first Monday of June)
Labour Day (fourth Monday of October)

Most shops and attractions are closed on Christmas Day, Good Friday and the morning of Anzac Day. Tourist amenities are usually open on the other public holidays.

In addition to these national public holidays, there are regional holidays which correspond to the founding days of each of the country's 13 provinces. The main ones are as follows:

Wellington region: the third Monday in January
Auckland, Bay of Islands, Rotorua and Taupo: fourth Monday in January
Christchurch: during 'Carnival Week' in November
Queenstown and Dunedin: third Monday of March

Annual Events and Festivals

January
Auckland: Yachting Regatta (fourth Monday of January). The world's largest sailing regatta is held at Auckland harbour.

February
Marlborough: Wine & Food Festival at Blenheim (second weekend).

February/March
Wellington: Biennial (in even years) International Festival of the Arts.

March
Hokitika: Wild Food Festival (first or second weekend).
Masterton: Golden Shears Sheep Shearing Competition.

Easter
Hastings: Highland Games.

April
Wanaka: Warbirds over Wanaka aviation show (odd years).

June
Hamilton: National Agricultural Field Days held over four days at Mystery Creek; this is one of the world's largest agricultural shows (second week).
Queenstown: The town celebrates the opening of its ski season with its Fun Festival (second half of June).

September
Alexandra: Blossom Festival.

October
New Plymouth: Rhododendron Festival takes place for a fortnight in October.

November
Auckland: Ellerslie Garden Show for five days (second week).
Christchurch: Show Week and horse-racing carnival mid-November.
Countrywide: Guy Fawkes evening fireworks on 5 November.

December
Timaru: Caroline Bay Christmas Carnival.

Practical Matters

TIME DIFFERENCES

GMT
12 noon

New Zealand
12 midnight

Germany
1PM

USA (NY)
7AM

Netherlands
1PM

Spain
1PM

BEFORE YOU GO

WHAT YOU NEED

● Required
○ Suggested
▲ Not required

	UK	Germany	USA	Netherlands	Spain
Passport (must be valid for 3 months beyond period of stay)	●	●	●	●	●
Visa (for holiday travel up to 3 months)	▲	▲	▲	▲	▲
Onward or Return Ticket	●	●	●	●	●
Health Inoculations	▲	▲	▲	▲	▲
Health Documentation (➤ 123, Health)	○	○	○	○	○
Travel Insurance	○	○	○	○	○
Driving Licence (national, International for Spanish nationals)	●	●	●	●	●
Car Insurance Certificate (included if car is rented)	▲	▲	▲	▲	▲
Car Registration Document	▲	▲	▲	▲	▲

WHEN TO GO

Auckland

▨ High season
▢ Low season

23°C	23°C	22°C	20°C	18°C	15°C	13°C	14°C	16°C	18°C	19°C	22°C
JAN	FEB	MAR	APR	MAY	JUN	JUL	AUG	SEP	OCT	NOV	DEC

☀ Very wet   ☁ Wet   ☁ Cloud   ☀ Sun   ⛅ Showers/Sun

TOURIST OFFICES

In the UK
New Zealand Tourism Board
New Zealand House
80 Haymarket
London SW1Y 4TQ
☎ 0839 300 900 (recorded information charged at 39p per minute cheap rate, 49p per minute peak rate)

In the USA
New Zealand Tourist Board
Suite 300, Santa Monica Boulevard
Santa Monica
California
CA90401
☎ 310/395 7480
Fax: 310/395 5453

POLICE 111

FIRE 111

AMBULANCE 111

WHEN YOU ARE THERE

ARRIVING

Most visitors arrive by air, through the three main international airports of Auckland, Wellington and Christchurch. Auckland is the largest gateway, served by more than 20 airlines. Air New Zealand is the national airline (☎ 09 366 2400).

Auckland, North Island Kilometres to city centre	Journey times	
	🚆	N/A
23 kilometres	🚌	40 minutes
	🚗	30 minutes

Christchurch, South Island Kilometres to city centre	Journey times	
	🚆	N/A
11 kilometres	🚌	30 minutes
	🚗	20 minutes

MONEY

New Zealand currency is decimal based and divided into dollars and cents. The New Zealand dollar is not tied to any other currency. Coins now in circulation are in denominations of 5, 10, 20 and 50 cents and in 1 or 2 dollars. Notes are in denominations of 5, 10, 20, 50 and 100 dollars.
There is no limit to the amount of NZ dollars that may be brought into or taken out of the country.
Credit cards are widely accepted and include Mastercard, Visa, American Express and Diners Club, and travellers cheques can be changed at banks and Change Bureaux in all towns.

TIME

 New Zealand is 12 hours ahead of Greenwich Mean Time (GMT+12). New Zealand's proximity to the International Date Line makes it one of the first countries to see each new day.

CUSTOMS

 YES

There are specific allowances for the import of alcohol, cigarettes and luxury goods into the country for those over 17 years of age:
Alcohol:
  spirits: 1.125L
  wine: 4.5L *or*
  beer: 4.5L
Cigarettes: 200 *or*
Cigars: 50 *or*
Tobacco: 250 grams
Toilet water: not specified

Gifts of combined value of NZ$700 or over should be declared and will be subject to customs duty and Goods and Services Tax.

You will be issued on the flight with Passenger Arrival Papers, including an Agriculture Quarantine form.

 NO

Non-prescription drugs, animal, plant or other food products. New Zealand is strict about protecting its agriculture and the interior of the aircraft will be sprayed on arrival.

CONSULATES

				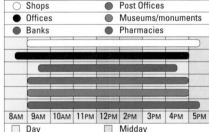
UK ☎ 09 303 2973	**Germany** ☎ 09 377 3460	**USA** ☎ 09 303 2724	**Netherlands** ☎ 09 473 8652	**Spain** (Embassy in Australia) ☎ 0061 6 273 555

WHEN YOU ARE THERE

TOURIST OFFICES

- **New Zealand Tourism Board**
  P O Box 95
  Lambton Quay
  Wellington
  ☎ 04 472 8860
  Fax: 04 478 1736

Tourist Offices

- **Auckland**
  299 Queen Street
  Aotea Square
  ☎ 09 366 6888

- **Wellington**
  City Visitor Information Centre
  Civic Administration Building
  Corner Wakefield and Victoria Street
  ☎ 04 801 4000

- **Rotorua**
  Tourism Rotorua Complex
  67 Fenton Street
  ☎ 07 348 5179

- **Christchurch**
  Information Centre
  Christchurch Arts Centre
  ☎ 03 366 0989

Over 70 tourist offices throughout the country form the Visitor Information Network, co-ordinated by the New Zealand Tourist Board. Because they are linked in one network, Visitor Information Centres can also access information on areas other than their own. They provide an invaluable, up-to-date service and should be your first port of call.

NATIONAL HOLIDAYS

J	F	M	A	M	J	J	A	S	O	N	D
2	1	(2)	1(3)		1				1		2

1–2 Jan	New Year
6 Feb	Waitangi Day
Mar/Apr	Good Friday
Mar/Apr	Easter Monday
25 Apr	ANZAC Day
Jun (first Mon)	Queen's Birthday
Oct (fourth Mon)	Labour Day
25 Dec	Christmas Day
26 Dec	Boxing Day

In addition, each of the regions of New Zealand has an Anniversary day, the date of which is decided each year.

Some shops and attractions will be open on all but Christmas Day, Good Friday, and ANZAC Day.

OPENING HOURS

○ Shops	● Post Offices
● Offices	● Museums/monuments
● Banks	● Pharmacies

8AM	9AM	10AM	11PM	12PM	2PM	3PM	4PM	5PM

☐ Day	☐ Midday
☐ Evening	

In addition to the above, pharmacies and shops are open on Saturday from 9–12 or 9–4 and some shops are open on Sunday. The bigger towns usually have late-night shopping on Thursday or Friday until 8:30 or 9PM. Some smaller shops close at lunchtime on Saturdays. Local convenience stores ('dairies') are usually open from 7AM to 10PM seven days a week.

Times of museum opening vary and many are open at weekends, too – for details see individual museums listed in the What to See section of this guide.

**DRIVE ON THE
LEFT**

**TOILETS
FREE**

PUBLIC TRANSPORT

Internal Flights Air New Zealand and Ansett New Zealand fly the principal routes within the country and together link about 30 destinations. Both airlines offer an Air Pass scheme which must be bought before travelling to New Zealand but can be open-dated.

Trains The New Zealand railway system, run by Tranz Rail, operates long-distance trains with daily services between the main centres, and the Coastal Pacific and TranzAlpine Express (► 24). There are various travel passes available, which allow travel on ferries operated by the railways, and on Inter City coachlines. Reservations ☎ 0800 802 802.

Island Buses The Inter City bus network (☎ 09 357 8400) covers much of the country, including many of the tourist areas. Newmans Coachlines, in the North Island, operate all major routes, and Mount Cook Line operates all the major South Island Routes.

Ferries The inter-island ferry service is operated by Tranz Rail (☎ 0800 802 802). It is a roll-on roll-off service carrying passengers, motor vehicles and railway wagons. There are five return sailings from Wellington to Picton each day, taking 3 hours 20 minutes each way.

Urban Transport Christchurch has a modern tramway system and Auckland has a good bus network, including tourist buses which shuttle around the widely spread attractions of the city. Wellington is a major transport centre and ferry terminal, with a cable car from downtown to the upper slopes of the Kelburn area. In some cities bus fares are reduced in off-peak hours Mon–Fri. Cyclists are well provided for.

CAR RENTAL

All the major rental firms are represented in New Zealand. You must be at least 21 to rent a car or motorhome. For inter-island travel, many companies require you to leave the vehicle on one island and pick up another on leaving the ferry. One-way rentals can also be arranged.

TAXIS

Taxis can be hired from ranks; they do not cruise and cannot be flagged down. In some towns taxis even offer a rate cheaper than a bus service. For long-distance journeys negotiate the fare in advance.
You are not expected to tip taxi drivers.

DRIVING

Speed limits on motorways: **100kph**

Speed limits on main roads: **100kph**

Speed limits on urban roads: **50kph**

Must be worn in front seats at all times and in rear seats where fitted.

Random breath and blood testing. Limit: 80mg of alcohol in 100ml of blood. For drivers under 21 the limit is zero.

Petrol comes in two grades: unleaded 96 octane and unleaded 91 octane. Diesel is also available. LPG (liquified petroleum gas) and CNG (compressed natural gas) are also available (CNG not in the South Island). In rural areas service stations may be scarce and may be closed at weekends or outside normal hours. Major centres have 24-hour stations.

There are plenty of motor garages and service stations throughout the country and most rental companies include a free breakdown service as part of the hire package. Automobile Association members receive free reciprocal membership of the New Zealand AA, including breakdown assistance, maps and accommodation guides (☎ 09 377 4660, Fax: 09 309 4563).

PERSONAL SAFETY

There is an efficient police force modelled on the British system. Police do not carry arms. Whilst New Zealand is a generally safe society, the usual common-sense precautions should be taken to ensure personal safety:

- Avoid walking alone in dark areas of towns.
- If walking in bush or mountain country, take good maps, dress sensibly, take supplies of food and drink, and tell someone what your plans are.
- Beware of pickpockets.
- Do not leave valuables in unattended cars.

Police assistance:
☎ **111**
from any call box

TELEPHONES

Telecom operate the public telephone service in New Zealand. Most public call boxes use Telecom phone cards, available in dairies (general stores) and other shops.

For Directory Enquiries dial 018, International Directory Enquires dial 0172.

International Dialling Codes	
From New Zealand to:	
UK:	**00 44**
Germany:	**00 49**
USA:	**00 1**
Netherlands:	**00 31**
Spain:	**00 34**

POST

Post Offices
The logo for NZ Post Limited is a stylised envelope. It is an efficient service with two grades of post for letters and parcels: Standard Post (for surface mail) and Fastpost (usually airmail). There are Post Shops in most large towns selling stamps, postcards and stationery.
🕒 Mon–Fri 9–5PM

ELECTRICITY

The power supply in New Zealand is: 230–40 volts AC.

Sockets accept two or three-flat-pin plugs. Hotels and motels provide 110-volt/20 watt AC sockets for shavers only. An adaptor will be required for those appliances which do not operate on 230 volts.

TIPS/GRATUITIES

Yes ✓   No ✗

Tipping is not generally expected in New Zealand, although it will not be refused if you wish to reward exceptional service.

Restaurants (GST is added to bill)	✗
Tour guides	✗
Hairdressers	✗
Taxi drivers	✗
Chambermaids	✗
Porters	✗
Toilets	✗

PHOTOGRAPHY

What to photograph: New Zealand is immensely photogenic, and the scenery breathtaking. Mountains, geysers, waterfalls and forests, together with Maori culture, make excellent photo subjects.

Best time to photograph: The air is fresh and clear and the light good all year round except, perhaps, when it is raining!

Where to buy film: Film and camera batteries are readily available in shops, pharmacies, airports etc.

HEALTH

Insurance
Some medical services are subsidised for visitors from Australia and the UK, but all visitors are strongly recommended to arrange medical insurance cover in advance of their trip.

Dental Services
All medical, including dental services, are of a high standard and addresses can be found in the front of local telephone directories.

Sun Advice
The most serious potential health risk in New Zealand is from the sun. Ultra-violet radiation throughout the country is particularly high. Take adequate precautions, even on overcast days, by wearing a sun hat and using a sun cream with a high protection factor. Always ensure that children are well protected.

Drugs
Chemists (pharmacies) are usually open during normal shopping hours. If you are on unusual medication, take supplies with you as there is no guarantee that they will be available locally. Take your prescription certificate to avoid difficulties with customs.

Safe Water
Tap water in New Zealand is safe to drink everywhere. City water supplies are chlorinated and most are also fluoridated. If camping in remote areas, always boil water before drinking.

CONCESSIONS

Students/Youths New Zealand is well geared up to cater for the needs of student and youth travellers. A wideTranz Rail has a 30% concession scheme for students on their rail, coach and ferry services, and Air New Zealand and Ansett have a space-available discount (50%) on internal flights for holders of International Student Identity cards. Youth Hostels Association members receive discounts on Newmans and Mount Cook Bus Lines.

Senior Citizens Tranz Rail and most bus operators have a 'Golden Age Saver' fare, with a 30% discount on the standard fare for those over 60. You will be required to show proof of your age.

CLOTHING SIZES

New Zealand	UK	Europe	USA	
36	36	46	36	Suits
38	38	48	38	Suits
40	40	50	40	Suits
42	42	52	42	Suits
44	44	54	44	Suits
46	46	56	46	Suits
7	7	41	8	Shoes
7.5	7.5	42	8.5	Shoes
8.5	8.5	43	9.5	Shoes
9.5	9.5	44	10.5	Shoes
10.5	10.5	45	11.5	Shoes
11	11	46	12	Shoes
14.5	14.5	37	14.5	Shirts
15	15	38	15	Shirts
15.5	15.5	39/40	15.5	Shirts
16	16	41	16	Shirts
16.5	16.5	42	16.5	Shirts
17	17	43	17	Shirts
8	8	34	6	Dresses
10	10	36	8	Dresses
12	12	38	10	Dresses
14	14	40	12	Dresses
16	16	42	14	Dresses
18	18	44	16	Dresses
4.5	4.5	38	6	Shoes
5	5	38	6.5	Shoes
5.5	5.5	39	7	Shoes
6	6	39	7.5	Shoes
6.5	6.5	40	8	Shoes
7	7	41	8.5	Shoes

WHEN DEPARTING

- There is an airport departure tax equivalent to NZ$20, payable on all international flights. Transit passengers and those under two years of age are exempt.
- There is no limit to the amount of New Zealand currency that may be exported.
- You should arrive at the airport at least two hours before departure time.

LANGUAGE

The common language of New Zealand is English. The written language follows British spelling convention, rather than American. There is little difference in pronunciation from one part of the country to another, except that in the South Island you may detect a Scottish accent. There have been attempts to retain and revive the Maori language in case it should disappear. Visitors may hear Maori spoken on the radio, used as a greeting (*Kia Ora*), and in place names. The language was entirely oral until early missionaries recorded it in written form. The easiest way to say Maori words is to pronounce each syllable phonetically. 'Kiwi' English also tends to have its own idiosyncratic expressions or phrases.

" Common Maori Words and Phrases

Ao	cloud
Aotearoa	Land of the Long White Cloud
Ara	path
Atua	god
Awa	river
Haere mai	welcome
Haera ra	farewell
Hangi	a Maori feast
Hau	wind
Hawaiiki	legendary homeland of the Maori
Kia ora	your good health
Kumara	a sweet potato
Makomako	bellbird
Ma	stream
Mana	prestige
Manu	bird
Maunga	mountain
Moana	sea, or lake
Moko	tattoo
Motu	island, or anything that is isolated
Pa	fortified village
Pakeha	foreigner, white person, European
Po	night
Puke	hill
Puna	spring (of water)
Rangi	sky
Roto	lake
Rua	two, eg. Rotorua two lakes
Tapu	sacred
Utu	retribution
Wai	water
Whanga	bay, stretch of water, inlet
Whare	house
Whenua	land

'Kiwi' English

bach	a holiday chalet in the North Island (pronounce 'batch')
Beehive	the main government building in Wellington
bludge	scrounge, borrow
bush	the forest
chook	chicken
cocky	farmer (usually *cow-cocky*)
chilly-bin	portable cooler box
crib	the South Island equivalent of a bach
crook	sick, ill
dag	a character, or entertaining person
dairy	general store
gidday	good day (hello)
good as gold	fine, OK
handle	beer glass with a handle
jandals	flip-flops, thongs
judder bars	speed bumps in the road
morning tea	mid-morning tea or coffee break ('elevenses')
mozzie	mosquito
Pakeha	person of European descent
Pom	an English person (mildly derogatory)
smoko	tea or coffee break
togs	swimwear
wopwops	the back of beyond

INDEX

Acknowledgements
The Automobile Association wishes to thank the following libraries, photographers and associations for their assistance in the preparation of this book:

ALLAN EDIE 122a, 122b, 122c; FOOTPRINTS (Nick Hanna) 7a, 24, 76; IMAGES COLOUR LIBRARY F/Cover: Lake Matheson; JAMES DAVIS TRAVEL PHOTOGRAPHY F/Cover: Maori; MARY EVANS PICTURE LIBRARY10a, 10b, 14; MRI BANKERS' GUIDE TO FOREIGN CURRENCY 119

The remaining transparencies are held in the Association's own library (AA PHOTO LIBRARY) and were all taken by Paul Kenward.

The Automobile Association would also like to thank the New Zealand Automobile Association for their assistance in verifying information for the Practical Matters section of this book.

Contributors
Copy editor: Rebecca Snelling Page Layout: Phil Barfoot Verifier: Michael Mellor
Researcher (Practical Matters): Lesley Allard Indexer: Marie Lorimer